A Recipe for
Bad Lemons

Ingredients for Success
from Life's Sour
Moments

A Recipe for Bad Lemons

Ingredients for Success from Life's Sour Moments

Angie Hundley

A Recipe for Bad Lemons

Copyright © 2020 by Angie Hundley

ISBN: 978-0-9990477-6-7 (paperback)

ISBN: 978-0-9990477-7-4 (digital)

For information regarding permission, write to:

The Zebra Ink
Email: publisher@thezebraink.com
The Zebra Ink, 410 Simpson Road, Rochester, NY 14617
www.thezebraink.com

Printed in the United States of America

Copyeditor: Sheila Kennedy

Cover Design: Jackie Zimmerman

Photography: Porscha Adams, Royal Photography of Leavenworth

Interior Design: Anna Weber

This book is based on Author's personal journey. She is not a licensed therapist, nor claims to be. This book is meant to share her discovery of how powerful the mind can be and is not intended to give medical/mental health advice or implicit/implied guarantees to results if similar practices are performed.

The names in this memoir have been altered to protect privacy. These chapters reflect solely the Author's perception of any people or events.

Dedication

To Grace, Jack, Luci, and Bryce.

You inspire me to be a better person every day.

Table of Contents

Introduction

WE ALL HAVE a story. Some path we traveled that led us to our current disposition. When looking at someone, their path holds so much mystery, which is why that old adage, "never judge a book by its cover," fascinates me. It's amazing to me how we can meet people and form some sort of connection, and never know "their story."

It became evident in high school that I wanted to be successful. At that age, "success" for me was defined as going to college, meeting a guy with a big family to fall in love with, and being a mother to four kids: two boys and two girls. We would live in our big house paid for by our undefined, high-profile careers, and we would take annual vacations to a beach somewhere. The typical young girl fairy tale. Unfortunately, I didn't take into consideration all the different paths along the way that would get me to THAT profound success. It hadn't occurred to me at that point that my definition of success would change over the years either.

In the first grade, my two sisters and I were removed from an abusive home and put into foster homes for nearly 18 months. During those 18 months, I faced the challenge of adapting to different types of families and stepping into the motherly role for my younger sisters. At age eight, I learned about abandonment when my birth mother chose her abusive boyfriend over me and my sisters. The only life I had ever known had been ripped apart. I gained a new set of parents and siblings, and sadly, only communicated with my birth sisters through letters and occasional phone calls. From that time on, as I grew up, I had to reach deep to find the purpose of my own existence.

Nearly six years after I was adopted, one of my sister's family invited me to live with them in a town a couple of hours away. There I would get the opportunity to grow up with my sister during my high school years. It seemed like a perfect plan as I got to be with my sister again; however, it ultimately posed many challenges. The six years apart put much distance between us. We were two completely different people, barely recognizable as biological sisters—her path mimicked our unfortunate statistic, whereas I still had an incredible drive.

My senior year of high school, I nearly lost my drive for success again after being involved in a car accident involving a fatality. To even be in a vehicle was a struggle and I literally lost all motivation. Naturally, I went through a couple months of a funk, before I decided to pick up, dust off, and keep going.

In the middle of my pursuit to find determination to complete my college education, I found myself with a surprise pregnancy. Years later, going through a scary pregnancy, and realizing all of the unknowns of my family medical history, resulted in finding a doctor who was proactive with my unknown genetics. That doc ultimately saved my life, and possibly even my kids' lives too.

Shortly after the birth of my third child, I was faced with yet another challenge: a divorce. As a young child, I went through the whole divorce process with my birth parents, but it seemed much different being on the adult side of that failure. That whole sense of abandonment was once again prominent in my life. I began co-parenting with my kids' father, and essentially starting all over again by redefining my family. I remember sitting in my empty home after the kids left with their father, curled up in a ball, sobbing with deep heartache. The divorce itself was tough but being forced to a schedule with my children through our joint custody arrangement was pure agony. Growing up, I never envisioned having to raise my kids part-time. Again, I found myself searching for a half-full glass in efforts to continue my drive towards a new definition of success.

Throughout much of my life, I have kept most of these challenges to myself. Most of the time, I pretended to live the fake life of perfection, but over time I realized that perfection is what we create within. My idea of what perfect looks like is nowhere near anyone else's idea of perfection, so why am I chasing the impossible? Over the years, I would meet someone, and we would share some of our hidden history, and each time, I was told, "You should write a book!"

Many of the great motivators of our time have frequently advocated to make lemonade of lemons and as I considered the suggestion to write a book, I sought to understand this concept to make bad circumstances better in some way. I wondered if my life had, indeed, been a journey of doing exactly that!

As I began writing the pages, I knew I had been able to look beyond motivational quotes, songs, mantras...I had been blessed with the ability to find the positive even when life did not go my way. I ultimately faced problems and learned to:

BE GRATEFUL—*sometimes for very small things;*

STAY CALM *when stress wanted to steal my safe spots—so I could reflect on circumstances and decide how to deal with them;*

MOVE "THROUGH" *major problems with a sense of grace, which gave me self-control;*

ACCEPT SOME THINGS *for what they are and honestly accept my feelings—whether they are stress, pain, loss—and know this is where healing begins; and*

FACE SITUATIONS *with the spirit of a warrior; dealing with whatever happens in life to develop more confidence and take on the "opportunity" with open arms.*

It's never been like me to be the center of attention or take the spotlight, neither in a positive or negative setting; however, through all of my challenges, or **BAD LEMONS**, realized I had the power to dictate each outcome. Yes, many of my challenges felt much like failure, but I always felt that each day was filled with a purpose. If today wasn't my day, then I could still wake up to a new day. I was privileged with the gift of mental power, to be able to look at a situation and find a way to make lemonade.

Bad Lemon 1
Family

Wear scarlet! Tear the green lemons off the tree! I don't want to forget who I am, what has burned in me, and hang limp and clean, an empty dress.

~Priscilla Denise Levertov
American poet. (1923—1997)

IN 1987, AS A six-year-old little girl, sitting in the backseat of my parent's station wagon and watching out the car window, my birth mother left me in charge of my two sisters who were five and three years old. She went inside the store to get a pack of cigarettes. Her clothes were stained and she wasn't wearing a bra. She looked rough, like a haggard 60-year-old woman trapped in a 29-year-old reality. She carried herself as if she were mad most of the time.

Honestly, I found myself afraid of her. She was extremely assertive and often physically abusive. If she spoke, my sisters and I knew to respond instantly, or we would be spanked with a belt. My natural orneriness landed me many hours of standing in the corner, with my hands behind my back, on my tippy toes. It wasn't ever a short punishment, rather a minimum of an hour. Many times, I would fall asleep waiting to be relieved. My birth father hated this punishment, and often fought with our mother in efforts to rescue us.

Our father was a sweet man, though I didn't appreciate that until I was much older. He was tall, slender with dark features, and nearly twenty years older than our mother. He was a hard-working, energetic man. He fascinated me by the many projects he had. A few times, I watched as he syphoned gasoline out of our station wagon to use for the lawn mower. "Make sure you don't swallow any of that fuel," my uncle would tell him. I watched out of sheer concern.

He would also convince me to do the wildest things. Once, he convinced me to take an egg from the refrigerator and put it in a nest we made, and then, we would stalk the nest for days waiting for a chick to hatch. Days later, it became a rotten mess, and obviously, no baby chick hatched. Another time, he convinced me that eating a fly would bring the tooth fairy. After a couple of hours, we caught a fly, ate it, and waited for this tooth fairy to appear. No tooth fairy came—just a sour stomachache.

As we left the store, my mother told us that she was taking us to a new home. As we walked through the enclosed cement front porch full of cracks, chipped paint, and boards hanging from the ceiling, I wondered if it would cave in on us. This "new" home was actually complete filth. It smelled very musty and dirty. The walls had many cracks and stains, and the orange shag carpet was stained beyond imagination.

That evening, my mother told my sisters and I that we wouldn't be seeing our father anymore. "He's mean and drinks too much. He will try to hurt you if you see him. He's a very bad man." Looking back now, I remember being afraid of him, yet I don't really know why. The constant negative things that our mother would tell us most likely contributed to these feelings.

She would continually use him against us. Once, after being typical kids, my sisters and I were fighting, and she reached her breaking point. "That's it! I'm going to take you to your father, and you know how mean your father is!" My sister and I were sobbing, begging, and pleading for her to not take us the entire ride to his house. She drove us to his driveway and scolded us, before pulling back out, and then returning home.

A few days later, my father came to the house, and they immediately began fighting. He was crying, "I just want to see my girls. Please let me see them!" Within minutes, the police came and took him in their car. That happened a few times before he just gave up and we didn't see him anymore.

One day soon after, an older gray-haired man, with a large belly delivered a washing machine to our door. As I watched him carry the new washer inside, something about him creeped me out. He kept watching me with his dark blue sunken eyes. It wasn't too long after listening to him talk to my mother, that I realized he was much more than just the delivery man. Within days, he literally moved in with us. This new stranger would begin to care for us at night while our mother worked at a local nursing home as a licensed practical nurse.

For the first few weeks, this new roommate seemed to be an okay guy. My sisters and I had fallen into a new routine with him. We would walk home from the nearby elementary school, where we would be greeted by my mom's new boyfriend and my baby sister. My mother had already gone into her work for her night shift, so we would not see her until morning. My mother's new boyfriend would make us dinner, which was always filled with gross peppers. Most evenings I would try to find ways to sneak my dinner in the trash. After dinner, my sisters and I would just watch television or play in our room.

One evening, I was playing with my sisters when my mom's boyfriend called me to his bedroom. Upon entering the room, I was horrified at the sight of what I walked into. He had his penis out, stroking it, and he told me he wanted me to touch him. For obvious reasons, I was hesitant and declined, but he was insistent and forceful.

Lord knows how long I was in his bedroom, as it seemed like an eternity. The whole time I kept thinking, *Where's my mom? Please come home!* Before he let me leave, he showed me he had a kitchen knife sitting on the bed. He told me if I talked about what just happened to my mother, or anyone, he would kill me, my sisters, and my mother. I remember crying myself to sleep wondering if I should tell my mother. *For Christ's sake, I should be able to tell my own mother anything!*

Evenings turned into weeks. Weeks turned into months. Months turned into an eternity. Over the course of the next year, many horrific evenings like that continued, except he would take turns between me and my sister. I never saw him do anything to my baby sister, but there were many hours my sister and I were at school, leaving her alone with that monster. He became more comfortable and confident with the situation, even bragging afterwards about how far he got inside of me.

There were times when he would force me to perform oral sex on him, and I remember my eyes watering as I fought to not puke. He smelled so awful from the lack of bathing and reeked of cigarettes and chewing tobacco. I wasn't allowed to cry, or he would whip me with a belt, so I forced myself to pretend to be okay with the situation. He was so disgusting, but I honestly was too scared to fight.

Each night, I could barely sleep; I had so much anxiety. Many nights I wondered, *which one of us is he going to pick?* No matter who he chose, my heart ached with pain and fear. Many times, he would pull my sister away and I would cry, worried he would kill her. Countless nights, I laid in bed through the entire night crying while wondering if I should tell my mom and would this stop if I told her? *What if I tell and then he kills us all?* Whenever I thought of telling someone, I had this rush in my chest. I worried that my sisters and my mother would be badly hurt, or worse, even killed, from my confession. I could even be killed. With all of those thoughts filling my mind, I stayed silent.

School was something I looked forward to, even though it was a struggle to try to act normal. At recess, I would see the teachers look at me and I would get paranoid with thoughts: *Oh my God, she knows! He's going to kill me!* I found myself making up random stories, as if we were all so happy, just to make sure no one would find out the truth. At times, the ideas of the stories really helped distract me from reality.

One morning, I was sitting in my classroom at school when the teacher called me over to her desk. She told me to run an envelope to the office for her, give it to the school's secretary, and then wait for her to give me something to bring back to the classroom. Once in the office, I was immediately invited into the counselor's office. Something seemed strange. Why would the counselor have something for me to bring back to my teacher?

The counselor greeted me and asked me to sit down. She kept asking me questions about my home. Instantly a feeling of sickness came over me. *Where is the item that needs to be collected? I'm done with this conversation.* The fear of what she might have figured out overwhelmed me, so I fought tears, but my struggle was real. As we sat in brief silence, I began to realize there was nothing to bring back to my teacher. Keeping from crying was such a fight as the tears started to roll down my face.

Her soft voice spoke, "You are safe. I just spoke with your sister and she has already told me about what's going on at your home." At that point, I was honestly scared to death, but the confession just rolled out with the tears. Discussing the forced nights with my mother's boyfriend, and even how he would kill us if we spoke of it to anyone. Even telling the counselor I was too scared to tell our mom and worried he would kill us all. In that moment, I was such a wreck, already worrying he would somehow figure out that the entire family secret had just been divulged.

My sister eventually joined us. We sat there holding hands while the counselor stepped out for a few minutes. The counselor was whispering to my sister's teacher right outside the door, but it was unclear of what she was saying. There was silence between me and my sister, but at the same time, the looks on each other's faces spoke a whole conversation. We ate lunch in her office. We even played a game after the counselor convinced us we would not have to worry about going home. For the first time in a long time, I honestly felt safe in those few hours, even though waiting with uncertainty.

That entire day was devoted to time in that room. Even though the counselor did her best to distract us from reality, I still kept wondering if the counselor called our mother, or even the police. Questions kept running through my head, *Is she going to be mad? Will he try to hurt her? Are the police going to take him away? Where will we go when school ends? Did the police pick up my baby sister?* Regardless, I was relieved knowing we were safe, and that our mom would soon be there to take us away from it all.

The dismissal bell rang at the end of school. After the chaos of dismissal, the counselor led my sister and me to the main office where my mother and baby sister were. There were a couple of police officers, and another woman, who introduced herself as Ms. Melissa, from Social Services. The woman was talking to me, but I was more focused on my mom cussing, and telling them how ridiculous the situation was.

She was so out of control with her yelling, and the situation was so embarrassing, and was acting so crazy. She never looked at me once, even though I kept watching her and waiting for her to say something to us. Ms. Melissa grabbed my sisters and me and instructed us to go with the police officer who was standing to the side. He put us in a car and within minutes, Ms. Melissa joined us.

As we drove away, my sisters were crying, and I remember thinking I needed to be brave for them. Even though I was scared and concerned about what was happening, it never occurred to me to cry, as my focus was on reassuring my sisters. We held hands and I kept telling them that we were okay.

Ms. Melissa explained that there was a nice family waiting for us to have dinner, and that we would stay with them through the night and possibly a few more nights. She reassured us that she would be checking in on us, and that we were safe with this new, nice family. When she said that, I had a thousand questions. I ignored my racing mind because I knew I had to continue to be brave for my sisters, even though inside I was a wreck.

The drive seemed long, however, within 15 minutes we pulled up to a farmhouse in the country of a neighboring town. There were chickens running around. A clothesline held clothes breezing in the wind. A dog walked around. We were greeted by a nice woman who showed us to a bedroom we would share.

That first night was difficult. My sisters and I all slept together. Part of me was relieved, yet part of me still worried that my mother's boyfriend would find us. As I lay in a new bed, I couldn't help but wonder what my mom was doing. *Was she kicking him out of the house? I bet she's so mad at him for what he did to us. Maybe the police have her in a safe home too.*

The new home did seem to be a relief. Our first foster mother kept her distance, but she was there at the same time. Our foster father worked a lot so there were minimal interactions with him. It was a little awkward for me, especially starting a new school, but my sisters and I quickly settled into a new routine over the next couple of days. We rode a bus to and from school. We shared dinner with our new family and went to bed together in one bed.

Nearly a week later, we had our first visit with our mother at the Social Services building in the town we left. The same lady from the school, Ms. Melissa, was there to greet us. She explained that our mother would be coming to see us, but that she would be in the room with us in case we needed anything. "You are in a safe place and I won't leave you guys alone," she promised us. At the time, I remember thinking it was strange that she had to be in the room with us, but then again what did I know?

My mom walked into the small room. I ran and gave her a hug and burst into tears. The confessions started pouring out again about everything that had happened with her boyfriend. She just stared at me in silence as I told her I was glad to see her.

Literally no expression whatsoever.

She did not smile. She did not cry. She looked possessed as she kept looking at Ms. Melissa and didn't really seem to notice my sisters coloring at the table in the room. Her demeanor was simply ice cold.

She finally looked at me, "Angie, I think it's time that you tell the whole truth. You know that your father was the one who did that stuff to you." The tears rolled down my face as I kept telling her that it was not our dad, and that I honestly **WAS** telling the truth! *Who was this lady? Where was my mom? I couldn't even understand why she was so different...so emotionless. What was she talking about? How could she have been so confused about what was going on?*

Ms. Melissa must have felt my anxiety, as she came over to give me a hug. She asked if she could speak to our mother outside the room. We all sat at the table in complete disbelief about what had just happened. "It wasn't our dad," my sister said to me.

"I know. Mom is so confused, but I don't know how to get her to believe us," I told her.

Within a few minutes, our mother and Ms. Melissa walked back in and sat at the table with us. My mom picked out some crayons and tried to color with us. She really didn't say much the rest of the visit. It was honestly the most awkward silence. Ms. Melissa kept trying to relieve the tension in the room, asking us about our drawings and talking with us. Our mom was physically there, but her mind was nowhere in that building. She just kept looking at me with this disgusted look on her face, whereas I just kept looking at the clock counting down the minutes until we could leave that room.

When our mom left, I asked Ms. Melissa why our mom didn't believe us. She explained that sometimes parents go through shock, and despite what our mom may have been feeling, we would continue to be in a safe place. It was honestly okay with me because I would rather not have to go with my mom and spend hours in the corner for punishment.

Over the course of the next few weeks, we met with our mother at the Social Services office. Each meeting was much like the first one. Not a lot of conversation, just small talk initiated by Ms. Melissa. One day, the tension overwhelmed me so much that I just started talking, "Mom, it wasn't our dad. It was your boyfriend. I am not lying. I am telling you the truth!"

She looked at me and said, "Well, there's nothing I can do about it now."

There was nothing she could do? What did that even mean? Emptiness consumed me as I could not even understand how she would say that she couldn't do anything about it. It felt like I was in a bad dream just waiting to wake up. I looked at Ms. Melissa, "Ms. Melissa,

I'm done talking to my mom today. Can we leave?" While saying this, I didn't even look at my mom, nor did I care about how she felt about me demanding to leave that room.

From that day on, rage set in and I refused to see our mom and was hateful about it to anyone around me; I simply did not care. My disgust over the situation became very obvious because I was vocal about the hatred towards my mother. It didn't matter who was listening—the negativity towards my mother spilled out. Sleeping and eating were difficult as I honestly did not care nor have a drive for anything outside of school. Eventually, I was forced to meet with a few counselors and doctors who would ask me questions about everything. By this point, I was overwhelmed with anxiety and completely shut down. *Did my recollection about my mom and her boyfriend really matter? Really, what was the point for anything anymore? Why should I keep telling everyone what was happening when my own mother didn't care? For the love of God, please stop asking me to talk about all of this!*

One day, a few weeks later, we got off the bus, and were put in a car where we learned we were going to another foster family. Ms. Melissa explained that we would be staying with another nice family; however, my baby sister would be staying with a different family. After hearing this, I cried, worrying about her not being with us. *What was happening to our family?*

Even though I cried and worried about my baby sister, I quickly fell in love with my new family. Our new foster mother was so sweet and nice to us. She had such a caring voice and made an effort to ask how I was feeling. She truly went out of her way to make sure my sister and I were comfortable. Our foster father was funny and caring. They had a baby who was around a year old, as well as an older daughter I enjoyed hanging out with. She taught me how to dance to hip hop music videos, which was a lot of fun. Many evenings were devoted to playing with our new baby brother and feeding him bottles.

My sister and I shared a nice big room and we quickly settled in well with a new routine. Visitations with my birth mother were still difficult as I still had no desire to see her. My sisters still went, but I refused to go. My defiance and hatefulness about going to those sessions kickstarted meetings with a therapist, which seemed so pointless at the time. Talking about a situation that didn't matter anymore was the last thing I wanted to do.

A couple of months later, my sister and I were once again greeted after school by Ms. Melissa, who advised us we were going to another "nice family." Next thing I knew, we were packing up our belongings in a box, and off to the next home we went. I cried in that car ride, wondering why we had to leave again. *Did we do something wrong?*

New home. New school. New family. We were there for a couple of months, and then again, Ms. Melissa, came to the house. The very sight of that woman had become dreadful! There I was, again, packing up my stuff in a box and going to the next home. This time, the transition was pure devastation. Before, when I had to move, my sister would be with me; however, this time, she stayed with that family as I travelled on to a new home alone. By this point, the negative energy between my sister and I was causing a ton of trivial fights and tension, which was too much for one family to bear.

Many days were filled with tears as I felt so alone. Not seeing my mother was acceptable, but something about not seeing my sisters was heart wrenching. We had been through so much together. They were the only ones who knew how I was feeling. They were all I had.

At that point, I had lost all hope for anything. Over the past year, my father was gone. Our mother seemed to care more about her boyfriend than my sisters and me. My baby sister was living with a new family and now my other sister was gone. Really, what was the purpose to even want to live? There were many thoughts of killing myself, as I didn't have anything to live for anymore. No one wanted me. Not even my own mother.

I realized I must have verbalized enough negative thoughts out loud, because I began to see more doctors who were asking me even more in-depth questions. A couple of appointments were in a room with a special mirror. There were doctors who could see me, but I couldn't see them. These "observations" seemed ridiculous, but I answered the questions asked, hoping it would bring me one step closer to my sisters again.

I wondered if all of these questions meant that I was going to have to move again. I really didn't want that because being shuffled around was exhausting. The not knowing from day-to-day where I would end up made me on edge all of the time. I didn't understand that all of the answers I gave were going to make their way into a psychological evaluation report that would be sent to the judge. Inside, there would be recommendations for my future, and I had no idea what that might mean for me. All I wanted was the uncertainty to be over so I could be with my sisters again.

REPORT OF PSYCHLOGICAL EVALUATION

Name: Angela XXXX   Age: 8   Evaluation Date: 6/19/89

Evaluated by: xxxxx M. S. Ed. S, Staff Psychologist

Referred by: The Honorable ZZZZZ, District Magistrate Judge

Reason for Referral: Psychological evaluation.

Texts Administered:

Wechsler Intelligence Scale for Children—Revised
Draw-a-Person Test
Bander Visual Motor Gestalt Test
Projective Storytelling Cards
Children's Personality Questionnaire
Jesness Inventory
Suicide Probability Scale
Multiscore Depression Inventory

Observation and Social History:

Angela XXXX is an eight-year-old white girl who is residing at XXX South Oak XXXXX. It is reported that Angela and her two sisters were taken away from their home about three and a half months ago for physical abuse and possibility of sexual molestation and placed at the foster home with XXXXX XXXXX. It is reported that after a while, children started having some difficulty, so therefore, they have to request for XXXX to be removed and put in another foster home, away from her sisters. Angela's mother, XXXX, is living with a boyfriend, named XXXXX, which they have been together for one year. She is working at the nursing home in XXXXX and her hours usually are at night which is when she is not at home, her boyfriend takes care of the children. Her first marriage was 1974 to 1980, which she got divorced because they could not get along, with no children from this marriage. She reported that in 1980 she married again, and her marriage lasted util 1988 with three children from this marriage. The reason that she got divorced was that her husband was abusing members of the family and that he was alcoholic. XXXXX is very confused about what the children are saying that happened to them during the time that she has not been home. She has not made any decision in regard to the report of sexual molestation and she still is living with her boyfriend. During the interview session with Angela's foster parents, it was reported that Angela has expressed felling of suicide. Several times she has mentioned that she is going to get a knife, kill herself, which they are worried about her.

During the text administration, she was cooperative and willing to take the test. She was well oriented to time, place and person, and there was no sign of any physical limitation. There was no sign of any delusion or hallucination at the time of testing.

Test Results:

Angela's verbal I. Q was Wechsler Intelligence Scale for Children—Revised, was within the average range (Verbal I.Q – 91), Performance I.Q. was within the Average range (Performance I. Q – 93); and her full Scale I.Q. was within the Average range of Intelligence (Full Scale I.Q. – 91)

Her highest score in Verbal section was Digit Span and Arithmetic which she scored within Average range. Digit Span is her ability to pay attention to the examiner and concentrate on what the examiner is saying. This also measures immediate rote learning and immediate auditory recall. Arithmetic evaluate numerical reasoning and speed of numerical manipulation. Her lowest score in this section was Information and Comprehension; she scored within Below Average range of Intelligence. Information is knowledge which has been gained by her on her own without having been specifically taught. Comprehension is generally a measure of social comprehension; a measure of common sense, ability to evaluate past experience and make judgment in practical social situations. Similarities and Vocabulary were scored Average which includes ability to form verbal concept, moving from one item to the next and adapt thinking to the needs of the new situation, learning ability both in terms of past or long term learning and in terms of accumulative learning.

Her highest score in Performance section was Mazes, which she scored within Above Average range. Mazes is a measure of planning and foresight, visual motor coordination, speed, combined with accuracy. Her lowest score in this section was Coding which she scored within Below Average. Coding a measure of attention, comprehension, capacity for sustained effort, visual rote learning, and immediate visual recall.

She identifies herself with male figure on Draw-A-Person Test. Her psychosexual differentiation is clear. The test indicates that this individual may refuse to listen to criticism and has a lot of hostility. She is very insecure and possible have severe anxiety. The text indicates free flow of basic drive and impulses with inadequate control. It seems to me that this individual is emphasizing on the past.

She has good immediate visual recall according to her reproduction of Bender Gestalt Test. The test does not show any organicity or neurological dysfunction. It seems to me that this person is having fear of losing control.

The Projective Storytelling cards indicate that this person has the ability to express the feeling. However, there is a lot of anxiety and hostility involved that she needs to express it.

The Children's Personality Questionnaire indicates average intellectual functioning. She seems to be a rather unhappy individual and even thought that she has the ability of expressing the feeling, but from time to time she keeps things inside. The test does not show any sign of thought disorder or any sign of anti-social behavior or thoughts. However, unhappiness and some depression are indicated from the test.

The Jesness Inventory Test indicates that she has a tendency to resolve her social and personal problems in a way that shows disregard for social customs or rules.

Angela XXXX   Page 2

The Multi Depression Inventory Test indicates low energy level, but no cognitive difficulty at this time. She has low self-esteem, but become irritable from time to time and also become hopeless and helpless.

The Suicide Probability Scale indicates a high score of suicide ideation and the total weighted score in this test indicates that this individual may be come suicidal from time to time.

Summary and Conclusion:

The Intelligence tests indicates Average Intellectual functioning. However, it seems to me that this indicidual is very much capable of concentrating real good and hving the potential of high average intellectual ability. Some emotional interference and possibly her environment effected her, causing her to not be able to produce a high average intelligence. The test resul does not show any organicity or neurological problem, does not show any thought disorder at this time. She seems to have a lot of hostility, insecurity, anxiuety, and difficulty controlling her impulses. She does have fear of losing control and even thought that she has ability to express feeling, but she is keeping feeling inside. Generally, she has a tendency to resolve her social and personal problems in a way that shows disregard for social customs and rules. The test result indicates that there is some sign of depression and this individual has suicidal tendency.

Recommendations:

As there was some suicidal ideation and sign of depression, a letter was sent to XXXXXXX and also the foster parents including welfare department to inform the of the severity of the problem and prevention for any possibly suicide. It was recommended that the foster parents can observe and watch her more carefully and also try to take away from her any item that she might possibly think to use as a tool for suicide. It should be noted that if this suicidal ideation becomes very sever, she may need to have help at inpatient facility to take care of depression and suicidal tendency. As tehre are some emotional problems evidenced by test, individual therapy is recommended for her to continue with Dr. XXXXXX. She would be able to verbalize her feeling with her therapist and learn how to cope with it, to prevent any possibility of suicide and deal with her environment. It is my feeling that Angela would not be able to function under stressful situation which may cause her to be suicidal. Therefore, it would be recommended for a less stressful situation and environment for her at this time rather than returning home.

In regard for recommendation for family, please read the letter to The Honorable XXXXXXXXXXX District Magistrate Judge.

Allen XXXXX

XXXXXXXXXXX Ed. S.

Staff Psycologist

XXXXXXXXXXXXXXXXXXXX
XXXXXXXXXXXXXX
XXXXXXXXXXXXXXXX

I didn't know what was in the report until years later. All I knew at the time was that I got to stay with the family

I was with and they didn't leave me alone much. I went to a therapist regularly and that seemed to help me feel a little better.

Nearly six months with my fourth foster family, I had a surprise visit from Ms. Melissa. The initial sight of that woman gave me instant anxiety; however, that day she brought me a new sense of peace. She asked about my time living there and if I wanted to be adopted into their family permanently. *Finally! Someone actually loved me enough to want to keep me. Why would I say no to that?*

She told me that my father hadn't responded to any paperwork, therefore, enough time had passed for the judge to make the decision for him. She also explained that my mother had decided to let us be adopted. "Your mother has made the choice to stay with her boyfriend, and the judge thinks it would be best for you to not return home." And just like that, at barely nine years old, my mother was completely gone from my life.

Ingredient
Resiliency

The yellow colour of the lemon is the symbol of happiness and optimism.

WHAT I DIDN'T REALIZE THE DAY THAT WE WENT INTO FOSTER CARE, WAS THAT MY SISTER EXPRESSED HAVING SOME PAIN TO HER KINDERGARTEN TEACHER, TO WHICH THE TEACHER QUESTIONED OUR LIVING SITUATION AS A WHOLE. MY SISTER'S BRAVERY TO MENTION HER PAIN WAS THE START OF OUR FREEDOM. THE INITIATIVE the

TEACHER TOOK THAT DAY PROBABLY SAVED MY LIFE AS WELL AS MY SISTERS' LIVES.

My sisters and I were all adopted but in three separate homes. It was difficult to accept at first, but the reality was that it was a much better situation for us all. I learned years later, that all of our adoptive parents were told that adopting my sisters and I together would be too much for one family to endure due to all of the psychological trauma we had been through over the years. We were fortunate that our adoptive parents kept an open adoption, to allow us to keep in touch with each other. A few times a year, I would get to see my sisters and spend the day or weekend with them. We continued to contact each other through letters and telephone conversations to each other.

Over time, our lives had drifted to our new families. Every day I thought about my sisters and wished I could be with them. It was easy to realize how taking on three young girls, who had been through such tragedy, would be a huge commitment for any family, so I had to let go of the possibility. Honestly, I was just grateful to be able to say I had a "home."

As time went on, I reserved all thoughts about our birth mother, as simply a mother that wanted better for her children. In my mind, she knew she couldn't be the mother that we deserved, so she chose to give us to a better home. That is how I described her on the rare occasion I shared my adoption story with anyone. By the time I reached high school, I started to believe that was the truth. I just wanted to feel normal and not think about my past. How could I not appreciate someone who wanted more for me? That was how I forgave her.

Often, I thought about our father, wondering where he was, and if he thought about us. In my heart, I knew that he probably realized that he, too, couldn't care for us the way we needed. By the time I graduated high school, my heart was healed.

As for my mother's boyfriend, he will, unfortunately, always haunt me. I wanted to punish him for what he did to me and my sister, but Ms. Melissa said that it would be too traumatic to prosecute. Ultimately, despite my choice, he got away with what he did, and the scars will remain a distant memory.

HE DIDN'T TAKE AWAY MY PASSION FOR LIFE AND SUCCESS; IN FACT, THE SITUATION HE PUT ME THROUGH EMPOWERED ME.

A few years ago, I visited with my second foster mother, and she literally sobbed when she saw me all grown up as a mother. She explained that she wanted to adopt my sister and I; however, she was going through some marital issues that ultimately resulted in divorce. She didn't think it would have been a good situation to put us through, so she said she was faced with the heartache of having to let us go. For years, I wondered why they gave us up, so hearing her explanation provided understanding and closure.

Thankfully, I learned I was resilient. I forced myself to believe that my mother wasn't the hateful monster who abandoned us; rather, a loving mother who knew she couldn't care for us. She gave us up for adoption, knowing that we would be in stable homes that could provide us with the love and support she obviously didn't have the strength to afford. She obviously needed a man in her life more than the love her children would give her. In my mind, perhaps one day, I would get the opportunity to show her that she was right; I didn't need her.

Instead of being angry with the situation, I found a way to appreciate what I did have. Having a place to call home was valuable. There was no longer fear of having to stand in a corner for hours over something trivial. Not only did I have two parents who actually wanted me, but I had food to eat, which was sparse before. In addition, I gained loving grandparents who spoiled me with affection. It wasn't long before I had friends who didn't even know anything about my past. Life was moving on.

Finally, I had stability, which I desperately needed. There was a new sense of freedom in knowing I could fall asleep each night in a safe home, without fearing I would have to pack up my small box of belongings and move to a new uncertainty. Words could never describe the appreciation of having more than just a small box of belongings. I had a bedroom filled with clothes and pictures on my wall to prove my fortune.

Bad Lemon 2
Tragedy on the Road

In biblical times, lemons were associated with hope, fertility, perfection, and abundance.

EACH SUMMER, I WOULD stay a couple of weeks with one of my sisters in her hometown a few hours away. I cherished those trips as I could spend quality time with t and make up for lost time. Her parents were very sweet to me and always welcomed me into their home. It was odd watching my sister call someone "her" mom or "her" dad, but that was the life we had settled into.

The summer after my eighth-grade year, my sister and I had convinced both of our adoptive parents to let us spend the summer together. It was decided that I would stay with her. Her parents got a room set up just for my stay. They signed me up with a local softball team, and even helped me get set up for volunteer work as a candy striper at the local hospital. It was such a highlight for me to be able to spend time with my sister again.

We spent that summer swimming at the local pool, riding our bikes, playing softball, and literally having such a blast. Anxiety consumed me as I started counting down the time to when I would have to return back to my adoptive family.

One day, my adoptive mother called me to let me know that they had decided to move to a neighboring town thirty minutes away from where we were living. Thinking about having to attend another new school and leaving all of my friends behind was pure devastation. My sister's mother told me she would like to help after I shared this new stress with her.

Over the course of the next few days, my sister's parents were planning to discuss with my adoptive parents the possibility of me staying permanently to live with my sister. Since my adoptive parents were having financial struggles, they were going to offer for me to stay with my sister and get braces, which I desperately needed. As we called them to ask, I was so nervous, yet equally hopeful.

As anyone could imagine, the conversation didn't go as planned. The telephone call ended with me in tears, and a plan for me to return within a few weeks as originally agreed. Foolishly, I had gotten my heart too set on the possibility of the new arrangement. The next few days were filled with tears before I started thinking about how I could convince my parents to agree and let me stay.

For many reasons, the plan to start over in a new town just did not work for me, especially knowing I just made friends right where I was. Also, I was really self-conscious about my crooked teeth and really wanted to get braces to fix them.

After analyzing it further, I found myself calling my adoptive mother and just literally begging for her to let me stay. Deep down she always knew how much the distance between my sisters and me was difficult. Their financial struggles may have also been a motivating force, knowing that they wouldn't be able to afford such necessities as braces.

Despite the love they had for me, it was no secret they were barely getting by financially. Thankfully, after a long cry over the phone, she agreed to sign papers so that I could stay with my sister's family until I graduated high school. After hearing them discuss their financial struggles openly through the years, I thought the new arrangement might be helpful as they would not have another kid to pay for.

Starting a new school, high school at that, was difficult, but knowing I was near my sister made it easy. Within the first month, I found a group of friends and began getting involved in extra-curricular activities. My freshman year I decided to try out for a singing role in a musical, which turned out to be my last play—I realized theater wasn't for me. My sophomore year I decided to run for student council. With just starting a large new school, I lacked the popularity to win, but it didn't stop me from trying again my junior year. My persistence paid off, as I won that student council election.

During my down time, I offered to help with chores to show my appreciation and gratitude towards my new family. After school, I babysat for a few hours in efforts to save money for clothes. My first major purchase was a pair of leather Dr. Marten shoes, which I still have. My first real job was at Sonic as a carhop. I split the income between saving for a car and purchasing new clothes, so my new family wouldn't have to worry about that added expense. Being able to afford my own clothes was gratifying, especially knowing I wasn't burdening my new parents with all of my needs and wants. They were paying for my braces, for which I already felt bad, giving them that extra expense.

Even though I moved a few hours away to live with my sister's family, my grandparents (my first adoptive father's parents) were extremely supportive. They would often come visit me and spend the day with me. As I got older, the visits were more difficult, as they knew I was working most weekends to meet my goal of saving for my first car.

During one of the visits from my grandparents, my grandfather took me to a local dealership where we looked at cars. Of course, right away, I fell in love with an electric blue sports car. We even took it for a test drive that day. There was no way I could afford to buy a car just yet. My savings account only had three thousand dollars in it, which was just under half of what was needed to make a purchase.

That very next weekend, my grandparents came back for a surprise visit. They were going to give me the rest of the money needed to buy the car that I fell in love with. Purchasing a new car was exciting, but I couldn't accept such an enormous gift. They were persistent on the car purchase, however, and we agreed to have papers drawn up from their bank, stating that I would make monthly payments, to include one-percent interest, until the car was paid in full.

There was no doubt in my mind they took my teenage promises to repay them back seriously. Honestly though, keeping my promise to them was my number one goal. Of course, the car was amazing, but my promise to them meant everything to me. When possible, I logged many hours to ensure they got a check each month, as well as having extra money for gas and auto insurance. Clearance racks became my new savings plan in efforts to be frugal with my clothing purchases.

That car was the highlight of my life. As any teenager, I loved my newfound freedom. That car took me to school, work, and even cruising up and down the main drag with my friends. To say I was appreciative of such hard work was an understatement.

One summer night, before my senior year, my boyfriend at the time had invited me to hang out with him and his friends. He was nearly five years older than me, which meant he could do many of the things that my age restricted me from doing. So, on many weekends, we often hung out with his friends at a local karaoke bar, which was fifteen minutes from my home. Even though we hung out at a bar, my time was spent singing, shooting pool, dancing, and playing darts. Since I would normally drive home, it was rare for me to have a drink.

On this particular late evening, his friends decided they wanted to go to the local casino to gamble. It was near midnight already, and since I was not twenty-one, going home was my only option. He was persistent on ensuring I got home safely, so he began to follow me to my house.

A few miles from the bar, we approached a stoplight on the highway. We were side-by-side on the four-lane highway, when I decided to be funny and challenge him to race. When the light changed to green, we both took off, except he left me about ten seconds behind. Obviously, his sports car was faster than mine, but it was still fun to be silly. Eventually, I finally caught up to him and then led the way laughing and singing to M. C. Hammer's, "Can't Touch This," on my cassette tape.

Within seconds, I noticed taillights flashing on the left side of the road. On my right there was a truck turned upside down in the ditch. *Oh my God, someone just wrecked!* Looking to my right, where the upside-down truck was buried in the grass, made me slow down. As I observed what was going on around me, I looked in my rearview mirror to see how far back my boyfriend was. As I looked back in front of the car, there was a woman standing in the middle of the highway. This woman appeared to have blondish-colored hair and she had her hand up, as if she were trying to get me to stop.

Seeing her made me instantly panic. In that moment, I found myself slamming on my brakes in efforts to stop the car. I let go of the steering wheel, which, with the combined force of the brakes, caused me to end up in the left lane of the four-laned highway. Before coming to a final stop, my car hit that woman! She flew inside of my car, hit the passenger seat, and then flew back out on top of the hood of the car before she rolled to the ground. It was literally a scene from a horror movie, except it became my nightmare.

Cars were flying past me still. It was obvious the drivers had no idea what had just happened. *What the heck did just happen?* In an effort to get more clarity on the situation, I opened the car door and looked behind the car. There were people running everywhere. My boyfriend was running toward me along the right-hand shoulder of the highway, making his way to me. I heard someone yelling, "Call 9-1-1. She's not breathing!"

Shaken up, I took my seatbelt off and stepped out of the car. The radio was still blaring loudly. In looking around, all I could see was blood and glass everywhere. Several people were standing over this petite body as I glanced down to the ground where the woman was laying. The thought of hitting this woman with my car sent me completely over the edge. *Seriously, what the heck happened?*

My boyfriend looked over at me and seeing me in a complete panic rushed across the highway lanes and grabbed me. He carried me to the ditch of the median and tucked me into his arms where we waited for emergency crews to arrive. It did not take long for the highway to fill up with flashing lights. Looking around and seeing so many flashing lights from police cars, fire trucks and ambulances, I felt like I couldn't breathe. Within thirty minutes, I was at the hospital. I couldn't stop crying and thinking about the woman lying on the side of the road; the shock I was in must have been severe, as the next thing I remembered was a nurse giving me a shot in my hip to help me relax.

The next morning, I remember coming in and out of sleep with many eyes on me. My sister and her mother were sitting beside me on the couch. My boyfriend was nearby too. It was an eerie feeling waking up to so many people focused on me. They were all whispering as if I was clueless to their presence. The previous night flashed through my thoughts like a bad dream as I sat up and went to the window to look for my car. The nightmare became reality at the realization that my car was not in the driveway.

After seeing the empty driveway, I went outside and sat on the front porch; my sister's mother was right behind me. We sat there in silence for a few minutes while I sobbed. "Do you want to talk about it?" she asked.

With bits and pieces of the night flashing through my mind, I remembered seeing the woman lying on the side of the road. "Please tell me that woman is okay," I said.

My world stood still in those few seconds as I waited for her to respond. She had tears in her eyes as she looked at me. "Angie, I am so sorry. She didn't make it. They rushed her to the hospital, but she was already dead."

Hearing this made me sob even harder. All I could think about was knowing I killed someone. The questions just poured out of me, "Why was she in the middle of the road? Am I going to jail? Where's my car? Oh my God! I just killed someone!"

My sister's mother hugged me and just started talking to me in a calm voice, "There are so many uncertainties at this point, Angie, but you are not going to jail because you didn't do anything wrong. The highway is not meant for pedestrians. The police have your car for investigation. Right now, you need to focus on your health and resting." And even though she was telling me those words, in my mind and heart, I felt so terrible.

Why was there a grown woman standing in the middle of the highway? I kept thinking of all the reasons she would put herself there. *Was she in trouble? Was she running for help? Was someone trying to hurt her? Is that why that truck wrecked?* So many thoughts flooded my mind over the next couple of days as I waited for answers.

Nearly four long days later, a detective knocked on the door asking if he could get some information from me about the wreck. With all the thoughts still racing through my mind, I just blurted out, "Am I going to jail? Why was she in the middle of the road?" Being in the presence of a police officer made me so nervous that tears poured down my face. First, the detective assured me that I would not be going to jail. He explained how he had interviewed several witnesses already and knew with certainty that there would be no charges, or any citations issued from the wreck.

This entire situation became extremely overwhelming but understanding more about the woman was necessary in order for me to process it all. The detective asked me a series of questions about the evening, and then he paused. He was silent for a moment as he gathered his words. He explained how he was a father to a young daughter himself. As this large man in uniform choked up, he explained how he struggled with the facts of the incident after interviewing so many witnesses, realizing how it could have easily been his daughter behind that wheel. He proceeded to detail out what he learned from those interviews.

He told me that the deceased woman was a 37-year-old mother of four children: three young children from her first marriage, and one child from the second marriage. She and her latest ex-husband were coming home from a music concert together, high, and drunk, when they wrecked their truck. They were arguing about something when they wrecked and proceeded to argue after the wreck about whose fault it was that caused it. She then decided she was going to flag down help, obviously, not realizing she was in the middle of the highway because she was so impaired.

The car with the flashing lights on the left side of the highway almost hit her, but they turned their car around in efforts to hopefully get her out of the road. Knowing it was too dangerous to get out of their car on a busy four-laned highway, they decided to try and get her attention from the side of the road. They were yelling at her to get out of the road when I came up on her and struck her with my car.

The detective proceeded to explain that after reviewing the science of the wreck itself, he was still baffled that I was alive. As he explained each possible scenario of the impact, he was convinced that I had an angel looking out for me.

He explained, that my slamming on my breaks, while letting go of the wheel, was **THE** only thing that saved me. He said if I would have swerved to my right, I most likely would have lost control and flipped the car, resulting in ejection or death. He continued to explain that if my car would have swerved the other direction, my car would have hit oncoming traffic, also resulting in a head-on collision death. And lastly, by letting go of the steering wheel as I slammed on the brakes, my car was forced to my left, causing her body to come into my car at an angle, rather than hitting me head on in the driver's seat, which would have killed me.

Hearing all of that was certainly devastating, but mostly made me angry that someone could be so selfish and reckless. *How could a mother put herself in a situation that left her children abandoned?* I thought of her children, and realized I knew that abandonment feeling all too well. Even though I was not responsible for her death, I could not stop thinking about how I was responsible for her children's pain.

Within a week of the wreck, I was notified by the police that my car was ready for release back to me. Since the car was in my and my grandparents' name, one of us had to sign off on the release at the police department. Since my grandparents didn't live nearby, it left me as the one to sign the papers for the release. Graciously, my sister's mother made arrangements for the needed repairs to make it drivable again. Since the police detective warned me that seeing the car might be traumatic, Seeing the car wasn't an option for me until it was fixed.

Of course, that car was never the same for me. The car that I worked so hard for, that once filled my heart with so much pride and joy, was the same car I later completely avoided. Even after getting the repairs done to make it look whole again, something about it reminded me of that horrific night.

The few times I would bring myself to get into the car, and attempt to drive, were unsuccessful. It had a musky smell from being left out in the rain while the police had it. Seeing the broken windshield glass pieces on the floorboard gave me anxiety. No matter how many times I cleaned the pieces out of the car, I was greeted with new ones nearly each time I got into it. That just creeped me out.

Over the days, weeks, and months ahead, I found myself hitting a serious depressive state. Unknowingly at the time, I was suffering from some post-traumatic stress, which made riding in a car incredibly difficult. While riding in the car with some friends, a squirrel ran out in front of the car which instantly triggered a flashback to the night of my wreck. I couldn't stop crying and wanted out of the car immediately. If riding in a car was unbearable, then driving a car was impossible. *What if I am a high-maintenance passenger in a vehicle forever?*

Ingredient
Power of the Mind

*Throughout the ages, lemons have
been used to fight negative energies.*

AT THE THREE-MONTH point of still not being comfortable to drive, it was obvious counseling was needed to help with my anxieties. Through those visits with the therapist, she helped me overcome the stress of being in a vehicle, and even more so with driving.

THE BIGGEST STRUGGLE, ONCE FORCING MYSELF BEHIND THE WHEEL, WAS DRIVING PAST THE SPOT WHERE THE ACCIDENT OCCURRED. THE WOMAN'S FAMILY HAD PUT CROSSES UP ALONG THE FENCE WHERE SHE DIED, MAKING IT VISIBLE FROM THE ROAD. EACH TIME I DROVE THROUGH THAT AREA, MY CHEST FELT LIKE IT WAS ON FIRE!

The power of the mind is so incredible! In efforts to remove unwanted anxiety, I trained my brain to be okay driving past that dreadful path. It wasn't easy. Many days there were tears just at the thought of actually driving. One day, I refused to allow that incident to control my thoughts and actions. That incident would *not* define me.

After feeling encouraged by my therapist, I decided to start tackling my anxiety by setting goals for myself. The first goal was finding a way to sit in my car for more than five minutes. Those five minutes turned into ten minutes, then twenty minutes, until I was ready to conquer the next goal: driving.

That first day putting my car in gear to drive was so scary. Tears flooded my face as I sat in the driver's seat, but then this overpowering rush came over me. *I can do this!* That day was devoted to driving around the block only to come back home in tears. I'm sure it seemed ridiculous for anyone to understand, but, for me, that whole block was a start!

My therapist once told me that beginning the driving process would be just like riding a bike. My first goal would be to start off small and build up endurance, or in this instance, distance. My next scheduled drive was extended to the store and back. Then, the next time, my drive was stretched to running an errand across town. Within a month, driving consisted of soaking up the boundless freedom I once loved.

My next goal was to drive on the highway, which seemed easy enough; however, my follow-up goal would be the most challenging: driving past the spot where the wreck occurred. For months, forcing a less convenient route in efforts to detour away from that area kept me sane. For obvious reasons, driving past that exact spot was heart wrenching, but I still determined that I would not cheat myself.

HONESTLY, WHY WOULD ANYONE SET A GOAL TO WALK TO THE TOP OF THE MOUNTAIN, ONLY TO MAKE IT HALFWAY AND THEN TURN AROUND AND WALK ALL THE WAY BACK DOWN?

My final goal was nighttime driving, and particularly driving past the spot of my wreck. It was time to stop taking the most inconvenient roads to go around that anxiety. That first night of driving past that spot was filled with hallucinations of a person in a white robe standing there.

The mind trickery literally almost caused me to run off the road. With those thoughts, I quickly pulled my car over and cried my eyes out for a good twenty minutes, before convincing myself to just drive home.

Many nights were spent driving past that very spot—trying to finally take the most convenient way of getting to my destination. Eventually, it got easier. There were a couple of times where I had arrived home and realized that my path took me through the very spot of my car wreck without even realizing it. Finally, it had happened; my mind and heart were finally healed.

By that next summer, nearly a year after my car accident, it was time to pass my car off to another grateful owner, especially since I had barely driven it since the wreck. Through all of the healing process, I had traded cars with my sister's mother, so that I didn't have to endure the moldy smell and broken glass pieces that continued to settle out of my dash. Even though I was mostly healed from that horrific night, it was still painful to be in that car, knowing its fatal past. Selling it was such an instant relief, especially after giving my grandparents a check to finalize the financial agreement we made. Finally, that chapter was over, and it was time to move on.

Unfortunately, my **INGREDIENT** would be put to the test again. Literally two years, to the date, a subpoena arrived in the mail for me to appear in court, as the woman's husband from the wreck decided to sue me for wrongful death. Complete devastation overwhelmed me in thinking about having to relive that entire horrific night through a court trial. At the age of 19, the entire judicial process was confusing. That entire night prior to the court appearance was filled with tears—I feared going to jail.

Thankfully, my employer at this time was a bankruptcy collections attorney in a law firm where I worked during college and high school. My boss reviewed the court papers and explained how people will use incidents like mine for financial gain. Given that the subpoena was filed on the exact two-year anniversary of the incident, my boss explained that most likely some hungry attorney probably convinced the family that the statute of limitations were running out for any monetary gain.

The attorneys I worked for at the firm were amazing, in that they made all of the arrangements with the attorney my insurance company had hired. Their immediate involvement essentially relieved a great deal of stress from the entire process, as it truly was overwhelming.

Unfortunately, I still had to go meet with the attorney my insurance company hired in preparation for a trial. There was honestly no way around it, especially as it got closer to the court date. My boss prepared me for the entire meeting and explained how there would most likely be gruesome pictures and diagrams from the wreck.

It was so surreal to be sitting there with the attorney, reliving one of the worst nights of my life. In recalling the events of the evening, it became difficult to fight back tears. Unfortunately, that was honestly just the beginning of the tortured meeting. Just as my boss had warned, here came the pictures that he had from the wreck.

My chest felt so tight while looking down at all these incredibly gruesome photos, literally being forced to see pictures of an experience I believed was behind me. The pictures revealed blonde hair being trapped at the top of the windshield frame. Blood smeared all over the hood. Pieces of flesh stuck to the leftover broken glass. Those pictures are forever burned in my memory.

Thankfully, my insurance company settled out of court, and it was such a relief to not have to spend weeks through a court trial. The settlement was so small that my boss was probably right about their need to collect on a stupidly small financial gain. As trivial as it was, my hopes were that the money I shared would somehow help the woman's surviving children.

Bad Lemon 3
Interrupted Goals

*Know'st thou the land where the lemon-
trees bloom, Where the gold orange glows
in the deep thicket's gloom, Where a wind
ever soft from the blue heaven blows, And
the groves are of laurel and myrtle and
rose!*

~ Johann Wolfgang von Goethe
German writer and statesman. (1749 –1832)

ONE THING THAT WAS ALWAYS CERTAIN TO ME WAS
GETTING MY COLLEGE DEGREE. FROM A SUPER YOUNG
AGE, THE CONNECTION BETWEEN EDUCATION AND
SUCCESS WAS OBVIOUS TO ME. THERE WASN'T REALLY A
DEFINING MOMENT THAT LED TO THAT CONCLUSION SO
YOUNG; MAYBE IT WAS ALL THE EDUCATIONAL DEGREES
WITNESSED DURING COUNSELING SESSIONS OR
REMEMBERING MY BIRTH MOTHER'S FINANCIAL
STRUGGLES. CYCLING OUT OF POVERTY WAS A DEFINITE
goal and GETTING MY COLLEGE EDUCATION WAS THE
FIRST STEP to ensure THAT SUCCESS.

After high school graduation, working full time
seemed like the most logical way to help pay for classes at
a nearby community college. There really wasn't a career

field that stood out for me at the time, so the school counselors guided me through the course selection.

During the summer before my senior year of high school, I was working at a part-time job at a law firm that a family member had helped me secure. Through the configuration of my college path, my boss had promised me a full-time job after graduation, especially as he could see there was possible interest in the legal field. It just seemed logical for me to take advantage of the career opportunity.

After graduation, I began communicating with the community college, in endeavors to get everything finalized to start college that fall. Unfortunately, the school required students to submit a FAFSA to the college for any type financial aid. The entire process was foreign to me. At that point, it wasn't clear to me as to which parents needed to fill out that form: the ones I had been living with through my legal guardianship, or my adoptive parents. The entire enrollment process felt like a game of scavenger hunt. After a long phone call with my adoptive parents to get all of the necessary information completed on the form, I found out that I would still have to set up a payment plan. There weren't any available funds for grants or student loans.

Much like most young adults, I obviously knew everything, but it didn't take long for me to realize how difficult it would be to pay for "adult" life while attending college. Following high school graduation, I was juggling three jobs just to keep up with all of the "adult" expenses. Sadly, still living at home rent free proved my level of cluelessness. My idea about adult expenses, at that time, only included a small car payment, fuel, insurance, tuition, and books. Obviously, my needs versus wants had not yet been established, let alone the knowledge of true adult living expenses.

The days seemed long. Get up early to exercise. Quickly get ready for school. Eat breakfast on my way to class. Leave class mid-morning and eat my packed lunch on my way to the law firm. Work until around 4 o'clock and eat another packed dinner on my way to one of my part-time jobs. Leave my part-time job between 9 or 10 o'clock to go home and work on homework until after midnight or later, depending on my course load. Sleep. Then wake up and start all over again.

After six months of this routine, exhaustion overtook me. *There has to be a better way for me to manage my time more effectively than to drive from one side of Kansas City to the other.* With those thoughts, I started applying for part-time jobs closer to home, hoping to save time and fuel. Thankfully, the persistence paid off and within a few weeks my two part-time positions was replaced with a full-time bookkeeping position at a local bank.

The bookkeeping position was incredibly boring. My days were spent answering questions about people's checking and savings accounts and preparing and stuffing monthly statements. It was also my job to run documents between all of the branches of the bank. Being the gofer seemed useless, but there was one positive side to it: the bank van keys were kept in the comptroller's office, and the guy in that office was super-hot.

Over the next couple of weeks, I had no problem volunteering for anything and everything that would allow me the opportunity to go upstairs, and flirt with the dark handsome man with dark eyes in a business suit. There was a discussion one day in my department about whether or not he had a girlfriend, but no one really seemed to know anything about his relationship status. Although, one co-worker did recall seeing him bring a female to a company picnic a couple of months prior, there wasn't any confirmation if it was his girlfriend, or just a friend.

One day, in a casual conversation with him, he mentioned that he didn't have a girlfriend. *Oh my God, stay calm!* My excitement at the revelation was barely contained at the realization he was single. For several weeks, I had been talking about this work crush to my best friend, so of course she received a call that day with this new update.

Within a couple of weeks, there was an after-hours going away party for a co-worker from the bank. As I walked into the party room at a local restaurant where the event was held that evening, there was an open seat at the same table as the hot guy. A couple of the folks sitting at his table worked in my department so making small talk with them might help strike up a conversation with him. After all, I was certain he hadn't even noticed me in that way. We chatted with others at the table, but there was no real direct conversation with each other.

About an hour into the party, my sister's mom showed up to grab my car keys, leaving me without a vehicle. While I was in the middle of talking about it at the table with my coworker, when she blurted loudly, "Oh, don't worry about a ride, I am sure he will give you a ride!" She was literally pointing right at the hot guy. Knowing about my secret crush, she winked at me, as my face instantly turned bright red!

Part of me wanted to choke her, but, at the same time, secretly thank her. To quickly shut down the conversation, I responded, "No, that's okay. I will figure something out." He looked up at me, and said, "Sure, that's no problem at all." *Well, okay!*

The party was winding down when he asked if I was ready to leave. We chatted on the way to the parking lot to his truck, then chatted during the ten-minute commute to my house. During the ride, we discussed a little bit of our backgrounds and how we ended up working at the same place.

We pulled up outside of my house and sat in his truck talking for over an hour. As I learned all about his family and college life, this guy seemed so amazing to me. We discussed my college and career goals, and even shared details about my childhood, which I rarely talked about. Everything seemed to click with him. *How was it possible that I was sitting in the truck of the bank guy I had been crushing on?*

The conversation was winding down, so he volunteered to walk me to my front door. It was a slow walk as we wrapped up our conversation. *I wonder if he will try to kiss me.* As quick as the thought came, I reminded myself, he was twenty-six and stable with a career and probably wouldn't want to go out with someone that was barely nineteen, and not even halfway through college. Within seconds, we shared a long kiss, followed by him joking that I would not be getting a raise.

The next morning all I could think about was the incredible night before. Walking into work the next day was nerve-wracking. Would he play it off like nothing happened, or would he even say anything? My heart raced walking into his office that day to grab the bank car keys, but was quickly greeted with a big smile, and his offer to take me out to dinner.

Over the next few weeks, we spent a lot of time together. Although we worked together, we kept everything quiet and professional about our relationship. He told me there weren't really any rules against him dating an employee, especially since I didn't work directly for him, but to be safe, we probably should not discuss with others we worked with. His job worried me more than mine did, but of course, it made sense to not make a big deal out of it. Well, it didn't take long for the new romance to spread around the bank.

One day after I arrived at work, he told me his boss, the bank president, called him into his office to confirm the rumors. He said the meeting was uncomfortable, but his boss confirmed that there were no rules against our new romance, and reminded him to keep it professional, which he already knew. We joked about how everyone at the bank knew we were dating before we even knew!

Even though we always kept our relationship professional, we both agreed a few months later that I should probably not work there anymore. After much thought, I decided to pick up more hours at the law firm to supplement the income, which worked out better for my time management anyway.

Over the next few months, we fell deeply in love. Soon, I met his friends and then his family. With him being the second oldest of five, he had a large family, which was something that I truly admired. We went to my family farm to meet my grandparents and adoptive parents. Everything was really flowing well, even though I was running nonstop.

After eighteen months of a busy routine of work, school, and romance, I started to notice how exhausted I was. Suddenly, all the energy I used to have seemed to have disappeared as I struggled to stay awake all hours of the day. It was early March, so I dismissed it as the beginning of a cold or possibly allergies.

One day, I was at work discussing my newfound fatigue with my best friend, Amanda, when she blurted out jokingly, "Maybe you are pregnant!" The thought freaked me out! I couldn't be pregnant. At the time, I was taking birth control and had too much going on to insert a baby into my busy schedule. Not only that, but I also didn't even have health insurance to go see a doctor about a possible cold, let alone a pregnancy! When I enrolled in health insurance through my employer, I opted out of the maternity coverage, knowing I wouldn't be needing that additional premium.

Over the next couple of days, Amanda's ridiculous thought was on my mind. *Wait, when was the last time I had my period?* Through my busy schedule, I didn't even realize that my period that month was barely two days long, which wasn't that uncommon when stressed out. After further discussions with Amanda, we agreed to grab a pregnancy test over our lunch break.

While standing in the bathroom waiting for what seemed like the longest three minutes of my life, we started to see the test change colors and immediately looked to see what it meant. Thankfully, it was negative, which was confirmation that I was probably just catching a cold, especially since my only symptom was fatigue.

A couple of weeks went by, and the fatigue had gotten worse. *It has to be the flu.* Every smell made me so nauseated. Each day was getting to be more of a challenge to stay caught up. When I had reached the point of barely being able to get out of bed in the mornings, the puking began. This is when it was obvious; I needed to see a doctor to confirm it was the flu.

After discussing it with my boyfriend that evening, we agreed to take a pregnancy test and rule it out before my doctor's appointment. There wasn't a lot of extra money in my tight budget to waste on a co-pay at the doctor's appointment anyway. When double-checking through my birth control pills, there were not any missed days. It just didn't seem possible for that to be the root of my new illness.

After peeing on the pregnancy stick, we started reading the instructions to understand the results that would soon appear. We stood in that tiny bathroom in his apartment, waiting for what felt another long three minutes of time, just to get the final result. He finally looked at it, and said, "Doesn't two lines mean it's positive?" Well, two lines DID indicate a positive result, which meant I WAS pregnant. We both were in complete shock. We spent the next hour researching online on how accurate that actual test was, still thinking that it could have been wrong.

Even though we just had a positive pregnancy test, we were still in complete denial. We looked through my birth control pills again, confirming none were missing. It just didn't make any sense. He was completely calm, and said, "Well, it looks like we will be having a baby." We both agreed that I should see a doctor right away regardless of the results of our home pregnancy test.

Within the next couple of days, I walked into the doctor's office, prepared to find out that the pregnancy test was inaccurate. After collecting a urine sample and additional labs, the doctor walked into the room and confirmed it: I was definitely pregnant. The confirmed pregnancy was one thing but then to find out, based on the labs, she predicted there was a ten-week-old fetus growing inside of me.

The room was spinning. Not only was the idea of a pregnancy overwhelming, but also at the realization that my first trimester was almost over! It was so much to take in. The shock finally wore off, and the flood of tears just poured down my face. There were still a few weeks to complete my associate degree, and I had just arranged to transfer into a nearby university to complete my bachelor's degree. *How am I going to be able to afford a baby when I am barely affording my current lifestyle, literally living paycheck to paycheck?*

The doctor was running through the entire prenatal process when she observed my flood of tears. She gave me a sympathy look and said, "Oh, you poor thing," as she gave me a hug. All of my anxiety poured out with those tears. She told me that a pregnancy isn't the end of the world and reminded me that so many women pray for such a miracle and never get the opportunity. She finished going through the prenatal instructions, and then as she walked out of that room, she again reminded me that despite my fears about the unknown, I was blessed.

After finishing up my doctor's appointment, I sat in my car in the parking lot to call my boyfriend with the news. He knew of my stresses about the whole prospect, and even though we both knew it was a strong possibility, it felt terrible to have to confirm it to him. Perhaps he sensed my need for positive energy in that moment, as he responded at the news with, "Congrats mom!" Oh God! Another flood of tears at the realization of becoming a mother. *What if I am a terrible mother?*

At that point, there were many motherly figures throughout my life; however, not one of them had been in my life long enough to help me understand what being a mother actually meant. My biological mother abandoned me. There wasn't a close relationship with my adoptive mother. Lastly, there was my sister's mother, and she certainly was a mother to me; however, we didn't have a close relationship either. It was unclear to me who or what a true mother was, as there had only been fragmented pieces of motherly figures in my life.

Over the next month, my boyfriend and I started to plan our immediate future. His apartment was much too small for a baby, and even though most evenings were spent at his place, my technical address was still at home. We quickly realized one of our immediate goals was to look for a bigger place to accommodate another human, a baby. So, the house hunting began.

Within a couple of weeks of confirming our baby news, my boyfriend had planned a special dinner at the same place we shared our first date. Since I only worked a few miles from the restaurant, he insisted on picking me up on the way.

Right away, he seemed different. First, he was sweating like crazy as he kept wiping his head with a handkerchief. After we arrived at dinner, he also kept going to the bathroom. On his third trip to the bathroom, I was just about to ask him if he was feeling okay, when he got down on one knee with a ring. There he was, in the middle of the restaurant, asking me to marry him.

Everything was happening so fast. Just last week I was attending college classes, and planning a career, and now all focus was on providing stability for a baby. We were interviewing priests in efforts to get married quickly, which seemed like the most logical thing to do in our situation. We were also meeting with the realtor almost daily looking at a potential home to purchase.

Neither one of us were ready to be a parent, but it was happening regardless. And over time, we both started to fall in love with this life that was growing inside of me. Meanwhile, as exhaustion came over me; I struggled to keep up with everything around me, especially my college homework. Keeping up with assignments was nearly impossible at this point.

Thankfully, the semester ended quickly, but with so much going on around me and inside of me, it made sense to put college on hold to prioritize for the baby. It was such a difficult decision to make, but the focus had to shift to benefit the current situation. Finishing college was my top priority once time and our finances allowed for it.

The next couple of months were dedicated to planning a wedding and purchasing our first home in preparation for our baby. In efforts to be closer to home throughout the remaining three months of pregnancy, I transferred to a job that was in town. It was a decrease in pay; however, removing the 45-minute commute twice a day was already saving me money. It wasn't ideal, but it was the best solution given the situation. Plus, the bills were piling up since my health insurance didn't have maternity coverage.

A few months later, my oldest, Grace, was born. There was so much uncertainty and anticipation with being in labor for the first time. There were so many mixed emotions following labor and delivery, but most importantly, the instant genuine love was truly incredible. Sure, attending college was still heavy on my mind, but being a mother was more important to me. And as my doctor had explained early in my pregnancy, getting the chance to be a mother was truly a privilege. It was my turn to give Grace the mother I always wanted and needed.

Ingredient
Determination

GOALS KEEP ME FOCUSED, ESPECIALLY ATTAINABLE ONES, LIKE FINISHING MY BACHELOR'S DEGREE. SURE, GOALS CAN CHANGE OVER TIME, BUT FOR ME, MY GOALS NOW AFFECTED MY CHILDREN AND THEIR FUTURE. HOW COULD THEY HAVE A PARENT TELL THEM THEY NEEDED TO GO TO A FOUR-YEAR COLLEGE IF THE PARENT DIDN'T EVEN ACHIEVE THAT GOAL? MORE IMPORTANTLY, IN THINKING ABOUT ALL THE FINANCIAL STRUGGLES WITNESSED DURING MY CHILDHOOD, MY CHILDREN DIDN'T DESERVE TO BE HELD BACK BECAUSE OF MY INTERRUPTED GOAL.

Of course, anyone can be successful without an education; however, my heart was already set on achieving a goal: my intent was to pursue my education, and settle down with a rewarding stable career that afforded me the time and energy to devote my children.

Throughout my years, each job worked gave me more and more motivation to complete my education. Being able to enjoy life without financial stresses became an immediate need. As Stephen C. Hogan once said, "You can't have a million-dollar dream with a minimum wage ethic." In my mind, being a part of a business decision-making team, and building career success, started with achieving my goal to finish college.

The first thing necessary was to tell everyone about my goal and my plans to achieve it. My personal form of accountability was being true to my word. It would have been too embarrassing for me to explain my commitment to something, only later to have to admit the plan failed. Next came an outline, detailing all of the steps necessary accomplish my goal. These details included what degree to pursue, which college to attend, and researching a college with a degree-completion program for non-traditional students. The last part of my outline included my repayment options since it wasn't in the budget to use personal funds.

I chose evening classes, which began a short time after signing the student loan paperwork. Some of my credits were lost through the transfer process, which forced me to take elective classes to fulfill the degree completion requirements. It seemed so ridiculous to have to take filler classes, but remembering my goal kept me focused. There was no need to get flustered with some formalities, no matter what it cost me. Determination to get my degree was my new drive. Through many years of promises to my children as well as to myself, it was now my only option. Everyone close to me knew of my goal, so it was time to roll. *I got this*!

Prior to children, being able to juggle a hefty load was a breeze, so it didn't seem like it would be too much to juggle again, or so I thought. The reality was that it was way more difficult than I could have imagined. Forcing isolation from my family, in efforts to stay plugged into my homework was so incredibly difficult, especially when there was laughter going on around me, and knowing I couldn't be a part of it.

There were times when it seemed easier to give up, especially with being so overwhelmed with keeping up with schoolwork, house chores, and my part-time job. *Was this goal really worth the stress?* To add to the stress, halfway through the program, we discovered our family was expanding with the news of another baby on the way. As with my previous pregnancies, this brought on an incredible amount of fatigue.

While sitting in my room one night in front of my laptop, I opened an email from one of my professors that detailed out a 20-page research assignment. Instant tears flooded my face while staring at my laptop screen. Grace, nearly six at the time, walked into my room and noticed my tears. She asked about my sadness, and I explained the assignment and how it had to be completed before graduation. She looked at me and said, "You can do it, Mom!"

While watching her leave the room, it occurred to me that she was watching her mother work for something. And even though she witnessed her mother missing out on the laughter and fun family time, she got to see what it is like to feel discouraged and still power through. She was right. *I could do this!*

My determination to finish my bachelor's program was what pushed me to completion. Nearly six months later, and two weeks before Luci was born, my degree was completed. Honestly, it was a relief to have it knocked out before being challenged as an ultimate mother of three children: six-year old Grace, three-year old Jack, and my newborn Luci. Phew!

Bad Lemon 4
Scary Pregnancy

*Lemon is known as the natural cleanser
that has the ability to purify things and
increase love.*

ATTENDING A COLLEGE FOOTBALL game seemed fun as I had seen the hype on television. My sister-in-law at the time invited us to come visit her for the weekend and attend a football game. My husband and I were so excited to soak up some much-needed time together, without our little one, Gracie, who was spending the weekend with his parents.

We arrived at his sister's dorm room, along with my husband's other three siblings, and began planning out our evening. We decided to soak up some bars in a nearby bar district, after the game. Since we had not made any prior arrangements for our weekend, we decided to map out dinner and transportation so that we could drink responsibly and enjoy a fun evening.

The game was a lot of fun, although I do not remember who won. We left after the game and walked to the bar district, where for a few hours we shared a ton of drinks. At some point in the night, someone from our group ended up calling a cab for everyone, since we had all been overserved drinking. Being a mother, it had been a long time since I participated in an evening like that, and the recovery for days after proved that.

A few days after our fun weekend, I went to the doctor to get antibiotics for a sinus infection. Within a few days of that doctor's visit, a nurse called to let me know that my lab results indicated a pregnancy. Of course, there were mixed emotions about having a second child, especially since we had not been planning for another baby at that time. Obviously, there was excitement, but at the same time we were worried, especially since I had just spent the weekend before partying and drinking, which was totally out of character for me. *What if I drank too much and it affected the pregnancy?*

Within a few days of our pregnancy news, I was able to get into the obstetrician to begin prenatal care. Since there was stress about the timing of the pregnancy, I shared my concerns with the doctor about any possible side effects on the baby. The doctor quickly explained that many women engage in restricted activities early in pregnancies, due to lack of knowledge of being pregnant; however, very few complications arise from those early engagements. *Phew! That was a relief!*

It didn't take long for the fatigue and morning sickness to kick in. By this time, I was juggling a full-time job, along with being a busy mom to Grace, who was two years old at the time. There were so many early evenings that she would watch movies while I slept nearby. She would wake me up when the movie ended so that we could rewind it and start all over again. The need for sleep outweighed my thoughts of being a terrible mother, by allowing her to watch movies for a couple of hours at night.

Grace was so excited about being a big sister. She often told people how she was having her own baby soon. She obviously didn't have a clue that she was about to lose her spotlight, though we did our best at keeping her involved through the pregnancy. We didn't want her to be jealous once the baby arrived. We even took her to a few of the prenatal appointments where she got to hear the baby's heartbeat.

By the time we had reached our seventh month of prenatal visits, my husband had a hefty load at work, so it was decided I would go to the appointment solo. The visit started off as it typically did. The nurse gathered my weight, which was dreadful seeing the scale change from the last appointment. She took me into a room and gathered my vital signs in preparation for the doctor's visit. Everything was looking normal, as she left me in the room to wait for the doctor to come in and finalize the visit.

My doctor walked into the room as he always did and asked me how everything was going. There were not any concerns or issues to address, and I advised him that everything was going great. He took measurements of my stomach to ensure the baby was growing according to chart, and then grabbed his doppler to listen to the baby's heartbeat. He put the device on my stomach and began listening as usual. He instantly had a puzzled look on his face, as he moved the doppler all around my stomach to listen.

He pulled the doppler off and asked, "Have you had a bunch of caffeine today?" The smell of coffee nauseated me, and soda was never craved, even prior to being pregnant.

"None."

He asked me what my diet had consisted of over the last 24 hours. I rattled off a list of food consumptions, none of which seemed to concern him. He then said he wanted to wait for ten minutes and check me again.

For obvious reasons, there was instant worry about his reaction. Before he left the room, I quickly asked, "Is there something wrong?"

He looked at me, and said, "It's ironic, as this exact thing happen earlier today with another patient, but she checked out fine. Basically, your baby's heart rate is a little faster than it should be. It might just be the position of the baby, so I'm going to have you lie down for ten minutes, and then I want to come in and listen again."

That long, drawn out ten-minute wait consisted of wondering what was going on, yet hopeful the baby had moved proving everything was fine. The nurse came in with a cup of water for me to drink, just a few minutes before my doctor came back in the room, as he had promised. He grabbed his doppler, and said, "Okay, let's try this again."

He placed the doppler on my stomach, and within seconds, his facial expression gave hints that he was not happy with the results. He took the doppler off of my stomach and told me that he was going to send me up the hill, to the hospital, to have them monitor me for a few hours. He said he had just sent another patient there hours before, and she checked out fine after an hour. Still unsure of what was going on, yet feeling like it was probably nothing, I left the office with paperwork to take to the hospital and started walking up the small hill.

Once arriving at the hospital facility, I called my husband to share the details of my doctor's appointment. Still optimistic, I shared with him about what the doctor said about having another patient earlier in the day that checked out fine. It really seemed like maybe the doctor was just being overly cautious, and that there was no real threat. My husband explained that he had a quick project he was finishing up at work, and we agreed for him to meet me at the hospital as soon as he was done.

Upon my arrival at the hospital, it was advised for me to go straight to the maternity ward, as there would be a nurse waiting for me. And there was. As soon as I pushed the button to have the doors unlocked, a friendly nurse greeted me, "You must be Angie." She walked me into a hospital room and began hooking me up to a fetal monitor. She was even teasing about my doctor sending his patients to the maternity ward for the day, just to keep the nurses busy, since it had been a quiet day for them.

There weren't any expectations as the nurse didn't really explain anything other than she would be checking in on me. As soon as she hooked me up to the machine, the baby's heartbeat was echoing loudly through the room. The nurse gave me the television remote and told me to get comfortable. In glancing over at the machine, as she walked out of the room, the baby's heartrate was fluctuating between 226 to 228 beats per minute.

While trying to find something to watch on the television, my husband walked in and greeted me. We chatted about the last hour leading up to his arrival and started sharing our curiosities about what was going on. Neither one of us really felt like anything appeared to be wrong. Even the nurse that kept checking on me didn't seem to show any concerned reactions when she looked through the printouts from the monitoring device.

An hour had passed when a different nurse came into the room. She introduced herself as the head nurse. She also questioned my diet for the last 24 hours, just as my doctor did. She jotted some notes down in my medical chart and continued to ask more questions about my sleep pattern. She asked if I had taken any medications other than my prenatal vitamins, which there were not any other medications. She studied the baby's heart monitor and jotted down more information before leaving my room. *Is all of this normal?*

This time, as she went into the hall, she started talking softly with two other people, one of which was wearing a doctor coat. I made eye contact with one of them, who must have casually mentioned my observation, because they slowly started walking away from my sight. I looked over at my husband, "Did you hear what they were saying?"

He looked away from the television to look out of the room, "No, I didn't, but I'm sure they are just getting routine information."

Something didn't feel right. *Why is there a different nurse asking me the same questions that had already been documented? Who were the other two people she was talking to?* Meanwhile, I glanced over at the monitoring system and seeing the same numbers, 227, 228, 227. *What the hell is going on? Why are we not being told anything?*

In the middle of my search for the nurse's call button, a different woman walked into my room. She introduced herself as a sonographer, and she explained how she was going to wheel me to radiology to do an ultrasound. *Finally! We can see the baby to confirm everything is fine.*

We got into the dark room and she began setting everything up. While she was typing information on the machine, I asked her if the ultrasound was part of the routine process. Her demeanor was very serious, "Only if the doctor requests to have it done." She put the doppler on my stomach and began to move it around, as she stared intently at the monitor in front of her.

In looking at the sonogram monitor, I could see my baby moving around, which was a reassurance. She kept circling over one spot of my stomach while taking measurements on her monitor. She was so quiet and focused as she kept taking images. She then stopped and said, "Okay. I'm going to have you lay here while the radiologist reviews the images of your baby."

While waiting in the room with my husband, my chest began to feel tight. "What do you think is going on?"

He looked at me, "I don't know. Maybe the radiologist will tell us."

Within a few minutes, the sonographer walked into the room with an older man in a doctor coat. She introduced him as the radiologist and explained how he wanted to get a few more images of the baby. In that moment, his presence confirmed something was wrong. They were talking in medical code back and forth, and then the doctor stepped out to go look at something.

The sonographer was again focused on the monitor of my baby as she was running the doppler across my stomach. The silence and intensity were making me feel nauseous. My own heart was pounding hard as my chest started to get even more tight. Finally, the intensity of the moment overcame me, "What's wrong with my baby?"

She stopped, looked at me, and tried to explain how she was just capturing better images for the radiologist to review with my doctor.

Tears were streaming down my face, "I can tell something is wrong, because everyone keeps walking around whispering. Can you please just tell me what's going on?" We just stared at each other for a whole minute in silence while more tears poured out.

She must have realized my concerns and anxiety because she looked at the door, and then turned to me. She whispered, "I really can't say a whole lot, but you are probably going to get transferred to a different hospital so they can look at your baby's heart. You will probably be staying there for a day or so, but that's all I can really say. Your doctor has to talk to you about it all. I'm not really supposed to say anything."

As I fought back the nonstop flood of tears, I thanked her for being honest with me, and assured her of my silence. She wheeled me back to the room where we had been staying in and shut the door. There was a bunch of talking going on outside of my room. My husband looked at me and the stress just poured out of me. Tears flooded my face, "I know something is wrong. Why can't they just tell us everything? We have been here for hours, and it's ridiculous they won't just tell us what's wrong!" He hugged me and agreed that we deserved answers.

With that, my husband opened the door, and he began talking to someone in the hall. He came back in the room a few minutes later and said our nurse had been in contact with my doctor, and he was actually on his way up to the hospital to speak to us. Finally, an end to what felt like unexplainable torture.

Within 15 minutes, my doctor walked into my room and apologized for not arriving sooner. He explained that he had been tied up with patients throughout the afternoon, but he had been in contact with the nursing staff for updates. He also explained how he had instructed the hospital staff to allow him to discuss the results with me, so that he could answer any questions we had.

He then explained that although he was not exactly sure what was going on with my baby, he felt it would be better for me to get transferred to a nearby hospital in Kansas City for further evaluation. He continued to explain that he was going to transfer my information to a team of perinatologists at that hospital, and they would be taking over my prenatal care until they released me back to him. He told us to go home and pack a bag while he got all of the paperwork faxed over to the hospital.

It was nearly seven o'clock in the evening by the time we left the hospital, went home to pack, and got to the Kansas City hospital. The nurses got me all set up in my room, hooking me up to all kinds of monitors for both me and the baby. Just as she was finishing getting me all set up, a doctor came into my room and introduced himself. He wheeled in a machine and began doing an ultrasound, as he asked us some general health questions. He again focused on my baby's heart and began studying the monitor closely.

After finishing, he explained to my husband and me that our baby had a rare heart condition called supraventricular tachycardia (SVT). The nurse would be giving me a shot of steroids to help the baby's lungs develop in case they needed to deliver the baby early. A meeting was going to be set with the cardiology department at the nearest children's hospital, at their earliest convenience, and that the rest of my pregnancy would be spent in the hospital under full-time monitoring to keep an eye on our baby. *Oh my God!*

During that conversation with the doctor, he told me I would immediately begin taking high level doses of heart medication, in hopes to pass as much of it as possible to the baby. To help lower the baby's heart rate, maximized medication dosages would be given to me around the clock. My blood would need to be drawn several times throughout the day to check the toxicity levels from the heart medication. Basically, my doctor would use the lab results as a way to determine the amount of each dosage without slowing my own heart rate too much.

My new six-week routine began the following day. The heart medication made me so incredibly nauseous, and the isolation in a hospital room left me feeling out of touch with life. With my new routine, I was allowed two breaks throughout the day to walk around and get fresh air, which was my opportunity to take advantage of getting outdoors. Many times, I stretched those fifteen minutes to thirty, just to keep my sanity.

A week into my new routine, during my morning break outdoors, a flood of emotions came over me. Sitting on the bench outside of the hospital, there were a couple of pregnant patients taking a smoke break, as their escape from their hospital confinement. Seeing this angered me, thinking about being stuck in a hospital with a sick baby, when clearly those women deserved to be there. They were the ones acting so selfishly with their prenatal care, yet here I was taking care of myself and the health of my baby.

That's when it hit me. *Oh my God, I did this to the baby when I was partying early in my pregnancy. I am the reason my baby's heart is so sick!* Those thoughts weighed heavy on my mind and heart over the next couple of days.

One morning, when one of the perinatologists came by my room for my morning visit, he observed my tears. Feeling responsible for my baby's heart condition, I told him about the concerns and guilt from my actions early in my pregnancy. He sat there chatting with me and explained how SVT was such a rare heart condition, and that there were honestly no known causes of its development, especially in pregnancy. Genetics could play a factor, but most importantly, my continued stress would only pass onto my baby, resulting in an emergency delivery.

From that day on, my focus and attention were on my baby. Getting myself on a better sleep cycle became my immediate focus. Before then, my sleep schedule was broken up sleep patterns throughout the day and night. That unhealthy cycle was replaced with me getting up early each morning and showering before the doctor came in for their early rounds. Family and friends brought books for me to read, as well as a cross-stitch pattern to keep my mind occupied. Keeping my high energy confined was brutal. I appreciated those around me who understood and brought me distractions.

My husband even got into a better rhythm with Grace, which helped all of us keep a healthy routine. He took her to daycare each morning while he worked, and then he left at noon to pick her up to come spend the afternoons and evenings with me. We would eat dinner in the evenings together, and even took Grace outside for my evening fifteen-minute breaks. This new routine allowed me to be able to read to her in the evenings, and then send them home, so I could go to bed.

The new routine seemed to help the days pass quickly; however, the weekends were still so tough. While being cooped up, everyone else was able to celebrate with family gatherings, birthday parties and barbeques. We even celebrated our wedding anniversary in the hospital.

After my fifth week in the hospital, I started questioning the necessity of my hospital stay and asked the doctor if there was another way to monitor the baby without having to be in the hospital full time. He was not really on board with any monitoring plan outside of the hospital; however, he did finally agree for me to come into their office three times a day for an ultrasound; my freedom was somewhat restored. It seemed like a great plan for me to jump on that idea, without really grasping the risk I was putting on my pregnancy. The goal was for me to make it another two weeks before my scheduled cesarean, which was four weeks ahead of my initial due date.

That first night back home, after four weeks of being confined to a small hospital room, felt amazing. My evening walks could last more than fifteen minutes, and I could finally breathe fresh air without a timer. Sleeping in my own bed at night and being a part of my family was so exhilarating. The most rewarding part was being able to be a mother again to Grace. We were able to resume our evening routines of playing outside, baths and bedtime stories, as well as tucking her into bed at night and making her breakfast the next morning. Being back at home also allowed me time to get the baby room all ready.

Unfortunately, it only took about three days before the guilt of my new arrangement set in.

During one of my daily routine appointments, I was paired up with a doctor who hadn't seen me but a handful of times in the hospital. As he completed the routine ultrasound, he said, "Your baby's scrotum looks a little large." Throughout my five weeks in the hospital, all of the doctors had been warned about me not wanting to know the sex of the baby. By that point, it should have been stamped all over my chart.

My mind was processing what he had just blurted out, trying to think of what part of the baby's heart he was talking about, since there was no way he would have accidently given me unwanted information. *Was he talking in medical code about the baby's heart, or was that a possible gender reveal?*

Either way, there was an obvious need for clarification. "Scrotum, as in the boy part?"

He looked at me, and said, "Right, but that's not uncommon to appear that way on ultrasound."

Still processing what he just told me, "So, I am for sure having a boy?"

He said, "You knew you were having a boy, right?" He obviously overlooked my shocked reaction to his random discovery.

"Remember how I didn't want to know the sex of the baby?" With me asking him that, he literally just stared at me quietly for a whole long thirty seconds, before he apologized for slipping the unwanted news.

That next day at the doctor's office, I asked the doctor what would happen if the baby started to show signs of distress during the middle of the night? He said, "Well, that's just it. There isn't any way of knowing, and my fear, is that we are going to do an ultrasound, and find something horrific, which is why you being in the hospital is the benefit to catching any critical signs." With that info, I immediately agreed to be back in the hospital.

Thankfully, we made it to our goal of 36 weeks of pregnancy, which saved us from any emergency delivery. The evening before my baby boy was scheduled to arrive by cesarean, the chief cardiologist at the nearby children's hospital came to my hospital room to go over the delivery process. He explained that my baby's stomach was full of blood due to his heart not pumping blood in and out sufficiently, and because of that, he wanted to have a team of doctors prepared to address his needs. We were told to be prepared for the possible need of shock paddles in case his heart stopped during the stress of the delivery.

The chief cardiologist explained how they would prepare to transport my baby to the nearby children's hospital for further treatment once he arrived. *I won't get to see my baby for days after he's born?* In thinking about being separated from my baby, I asked if it would be possible to get transported with him. The chief cardiologist quickly explained that my recovery would have to be in the current hospital as there wasn't room for me to recover at the children's hospital. Tears rolled down my face at the realization that we would be separated from each other.

One of the other cardiologists in the room could see my pain, as he chimed in, "That won't be necessary to separate mom from baby. I live just a few blocks from here, so I will just swing by here on my way home and evaluate the baby. I will also just leave my immediate contact info with the NICU staff to contact me for any emergency." Words couldn't explain how grateful I was for that man! In thanking him for understanding the need to keep us together, I gave him a hug of gratitude.

Sleep was not going to happen for me, as my mind raced with thoughts and anticipation for what the next day would bring. The realization of how bad my baby's heart condition was proved evident through the need to transport him to another hospital. So many thoughts flooded my mind about what could go wrong the next day. *What if my baby dies? Oh my God! He could die!*

My early morning began with a shower in preparation for the scheduled delivery. A part of me was so exhausted from lack of sleep; another part was overwhelmed with anxiety building in my chest, unsure of what the morning would bring. A few cardiologists and the neonatal intensive care unit (NICU) doctor came into our room to introduce themselves in preparation for the surgery. It wasn't long before we were in the bright surgical room, preparing for our new son.

Laying on the table staring at the large blue drape in front of me, one of the doctors announced, "We have a baby boy!"

My husband rushed over and kissed me, "He looks just like his big sister!"

The room was filled with machines beeping but still no sound of his arrival. *Why isn't he crying? What is wrong?* The isolation from the blue drape was overwhelming, as tears streamed down my face. The silence was killing me, so I begged my husband to tell me what was happening. He said, "They are working on him now." Within minutes, there was finally the first cry from my new son, Jack.

The cardiologist brought him over to see me for a brief moment before they whisked him off to the NICU. We agreed for my husband to go with them while the doctors finished sewing me back up. The doctor told me they would take me to see him as soon as I had finished the recovery process. Even though my mind was on Jack, exhaustion was in full force.

A few hours later, the nurses wheeled me into the NICU to see Jack. There was no way anyone could have prepared me for that visit at all. The dark room was filled with a dozen tiny babies. Babies tiny enough to fit into the palm of my hand. Jack, at just under eight pounds, literally looked like a giant baby next to them. Approaching Jack, I saw he had tons of cords coming out of him but looked to be nestled into his little cubby. Before leaving the NICU, I was able to give him a quick kiss.

After arriving at my final room, exhaustion hit me—hard. A flood of family and friends stopped by to greet us and meet Jack. At one point, the cardiologist stopped by to update us on his evaluation. By that point, deliriousness had set in, as the cardiologist explained his observation; my brain wasn't even able to process as fast as he was speaking. He may have been talking but his words were nowhere near matching my level of comprehension. After he left our room, my main focus was sleeping. My husband agreed to let me rest while he entertained any future visitors.

By the next day, moving around was much easier and I was able to spend time with Jack. Even though he was hooked up to machines, it warmed my heart to be able to hold him and attempt to breastfeed him. Still, seeing him in there was so incredibly difficult. The NICU doctor shared his x-ray with me, and that's when the magnitude of Jack's heart condition came to fruition. His heart was swollen to the size of his entire chest cavity. When comparing it to another normal x-ray, it was obvious that his heart had been overworking for quite some time. *I am incredibly lucky to have this miracle baby!*

There were a few times during those visits with him that his heart rate would go from 140 beats per minute to 240 beats per minute, which meant he was having tachycardia. It was heart wrenching to witness the nurses, and NICU doctor, insert medicine through his IV, to essentially shock his heart back to normal rhythm. Each time was devastating to watch knowing they were stopping his heart from beating, in hopes to reset his rhythm. Through each IV procedure, I reminded myself that he was alive and in the best place should he become critical.

On the third day after his delivery, the nurses were preparing for my discharge. All of my stuff was packed up and my nurse went over all of discharge instructions. It was such a relief to finally get out of the hospital that nearly consumed six weeks of my life. My home and bed were calling me.

My husband put most of my belongings on a cart and agreed to meet me and the discharge nurse at the main hospital doors. As I was being wheeled through the hallways, a gentleman passed by, all smiles, carrying balloons and flowers. *How sweet. He probably just had a baby too.* And then it hit me like a ton of bricks. Tears were pouring down my face, at the realization of leaving the hospital without my new baby.

Ingredient
Appreciation

AS ANYONE COULD IMAGINE that first night home without my newborn was gut wrenching. My initial excitement to be in my own bed was dismissed with a night of tears. Even worse, having to pump breast milk every three hours only kept the reminder flowing of how my baby was still in the hospital.

I FOUND MYSELF KNOWING THIS WAS DEFINITELY A TIME WHERE THERE WAS A NEED TO SEARCH DEEP FOR SOME INNER STRENGTH.

There is one thing that is truly remarkable about myself, and that is I don't stay in a funk for long. When feeling overwhelmed with anxiety, the first thing necessary for me is to grieve the issue, after which, I am able to attack it and move on. Sometimes it's difficult to even know what the grieving is really about, especially when being so consumed by myriad emotions.

So, the next day I stopped to think about what was overwhelming me so much. There was an obvious empty feeling from not having my baby home with me, which was a much different experience from my previous pregnancy. Recovering from a cesarean restricted me from being able to drive for a few more days, which left me unable to go see Jack. Lastly, it was difficult for me to understand his heart condition, still feeling like my negligence early in pregnancy caused his issues.

It is time to be done grieving, and start tackling my anxieties. My first stressor was analyzing the fact that Jack was stuck in the hospital, and not at home with his family. Obviously, there wasn't any way for me to fix Jack's heart; only a doctor could. With that, my mind started to feel at ease about where he was, realizing that even though he wasn't home, he was in the best place for his safety. Instead of crying at the sight of his empty room, or seeing his blankets, or any baby item for that matter, my thoughts switched to how he was getting healthy, and would be able to enjoy those items soon.

Another source of anxiety for me was getting up through the night pumping every three hours. It reminded me of him not being there. In visiting with one of the NICU nurses, she told me she would give me a code to use to call in to the hospital and get updates on how Jack was doing. It seemed like a good distraction to utilize my times of pumping as a way to get updates on him. My pumping time became a time to look forward to, knowing it was an opportunity to get updates on his condition.

As the medical bills started piling up, my husband needed to return to work, since he was our only source of income. It didn't make sense for him to have to drive me forty-five minutes one way twice a day just for me to be able to spend the day with Jack. In thinking about a way to get to the hospital, I remembered my best friend drove by there on her way to work. With that thought, I called her and asked her if she would be willing to pick me up on her way to work and drop me off at the hospital, which she was happy to do.

A routine quickly fell into place, which was such a huge success in easing my aching mind. My husband arranged to get Grace to his mom's in the mornings while I rode with my best friend to the hospital. This arrangement actually worked out great, as it gave me a good forty-five minutes to visit with her and talk out my anxieties. My husband picked Grace up after work and met me at the hospital, where we would have dinner and spend a couple of hours with Jack before heading home.

Near the end of Jack's second week at the hospital, his cardiologist stopped by to check in on him during my daily visit. We were talking about the number of tachycardia attacks he had within the last visit, when all of the sudden, Jack's heart rate went from 140 beats per minute to 230 beats per minute. As we both witnessed Jack have that tachycardia, we also watched the nurses prepare to bring Jack's heart rate down. As his cardiologist watched, it was obvious he was in serious thought.

After administering the medication to stop Jack's heart, the cardiologist's eyes got big as he blurted out, "This isn't working. Jack needs a different heart medication. I want to try something different." He told the NICU doctor that there was a new compound medication that studies had shown to be highly effective, and he had already seen positive results with a couple of his patients. He ordered the new medication, and we agreed to see how it worked over the next couple of days.

Miraculously, that special medication was the recipe to regulate Jack's heart, and his episodes of tachycardia slowly stopped over the next couple of days. He went a whole three more days with no tachycardia, when his cardiologist felt comfortable enough to discharge him.

There were so many mixed emotions about his discharge. Of course, it was exciting to have him finally come home; however, there was also a lot of fear about Jack having tachycardia, as he displayed no physical signs.

What if he had tachycardia and we didn't know? We only had a 24-hour window before his heart became critical.

Jack's cardiologist was phenomenal in getting us ready for our baby boy's new home. He gave us a medical-grade stethoscope and began teaching us how to listen to the baby's heartbeat. He advised us to check Jack's heart rate each time we changed his diaper and fed him. He continued to explain with an analogy we could understand...listening to the heart rate would be like listening to a song on the radio and detecting a tachycardia would be the remix version of that familiar song.

The cardiologist was spot on about his description, as the first time Jack had a tachycardia episode, it was instantly detectable. After checking his heart rate nearly fifteen times a day for a month, it was easy to establish a normal heartbeat. On one particular day, after putting the stethoscope on his chest, it was instantly a different sound; it was the remix version, just as his cardiologist described. That day, we realized that Jack had outgrown his medication dosage, which would become common throughout his first year since babies grow so much.

I had been plagued since the beginning of my pregnancy discovery, and my actions early on in the pregnancy continually weighed heavily on my mind. Despite two doctors telling me that it was too early in the pregnancy to affect anything, the concerns were still there, especially not really understanding much about Jack's heart condition. It was imperative to get more information about his condition to relieve myself from any guilt.

During one of Jack's routine appointments with his cardiologist, we discussed the knowns and unknowns about Jack's condition. When explaining my concerns and guilt, he quickly shut it down and told me there was no need to carry any guilt, as the two situations were not related. He also explained, that at that time, Jack's condition was so rare, the exact reasoning couldn't be established. He finished by saying, "When you think about every small detail that goes into fetal development, whether its eyes, nose, ears, or even organ definition, it's truly amazing that there are not more things wrong with babies."

In thinking about what he just said, my thoughts about a pregnancy quickly shifted, as he was right. *There is so much that goes into the development of a baby; it truly is miraculous that more things don't go wrong, all of which, are taken for granted. I am done carrying guilt!*

We were told that Jack had a fifty percent chance of outgrowing his heart condition before his first birthday, which, unfortunately, wasn't the case for him. If he didn't meet that milestone, then he had a second chance before his third birthday. When he was two years old, we took him off all of his heart medications to see how he reacted, and thankfully that marked the end of his heart condition.

He still had routine visits until his thirteenth birthday. We were grateful to have him monitored by the exact cardiologist that took over his care in the NICU. At that final visit, his doctor released him and told Jack he was essentially free from his condition, although he needed to remember he would always carry his history of it. Occasionally, around the anniversary of my long hospital stay, it's easy to remind Jack about the long days endured in the hospital, in efforts to make sure he made it into the world. It's still a little bond that we share, which is easy to tease him about when he wants to be a typical teenage boy.

Although it was an incredibly stressful time, it has made me appreciate my ability to create healthy babies.

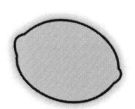

Bad Lemon 5

Redefining Relationship

It's not what happens to you, but how you handle it. If Life gives you lemons, make lemonade. If the lemons are rotten, take out the seeds and plant them in order to grow new lemons.

~ Louise Hay
American motivational author. 1926 – 2017

OVER THE COURSE OF MY teenage years, marriage was something I fantasized about, especially when it came to the perception of what my husband would be like. In my mind, this guy would be handsome, family oriented, educated, and career driven. So, naturally, marrying a guy that held most of these attributes seemed logical, or at least my perception of what was vital to create a healthy relationship.

Just as many relationships start out, we were on a high, and spent as much time together as we could with our busy schedules. We met each other's family and friends. We partied. We laughed. We were young, in love, and naïve to some harsh realities outside of living in the moment.

Many nights after working and going to college, I found myself racing to his apartment to scrub it down top to bottom, and then cook for him. In addition, I was leaving him notes and cards to prove my words of affirmation. In my spare time, I would iron his work shirts for him and wash his laundry to save him time. Doing all of that was out of sheer love and trying to find ways to make his life easier.

In the beginning, there wasn't a lot of attention paid towards the little signs that would prove what a marriage would be like with him, partly because of my young age, but mostly because my heart was blind. For example, within a day of spending countless hours scrubbing his apartment, he would have it cluttered. Cards and courtesies were given to him, in all honestly, expecting them in return; however, the thoughtful gesture wasn't reciprocated.

In those early days, there was much failure on my end to recognize my need for actions beyond words. I was giving to him what I needed and expected him to return the gestures. Like most pre-marital assumptions, in time, I thought he could be molded into being the person that I needed and wanted. Changing him would fix everything and our marriage would be fine.

We were faced with a decision in our relationship, that perhaps, may have rushed us into marriage, not allowing us time to consider the reality of our differences in relationship needs. While he appeared to need words of affirmation and physical touch, my needs included acts of service and quality time.

After three children and two houses later, the dynamic of our relationship really started to shift drastically. We both supported each other for the most part; however, we failed to put our relationship first. The relationship was focused more on hobbies and our children, than on the commitment of our actual marriage in fulfilling each other's needs.

A few months before the pregnancy of my third child, my ambitious spouse decided he wanted to pursue his dream of flipping houses. Of course, at that time, as a wife, a busy mother, and a college student, that idea seemed ridiculous. At that point, we had a five-year-old and a two-year old, and we were still in the middle of a two-year basement completion project. In addition, I was also in the middle of college classes working to complete my degree commitment. Despite all of that, it seemed like the right thing to agree to—after all, he was supporting my dream to finish my college degree, so it only seemed fair to reciprocate. Adding another project to our marriage, in all honesty, was the last thing we needed, but the decision was made.

Right away, he found a foreclosure about 15 minutes from our house. The excitement of the project set in for him, and he was eager to begin the grueling remodel. The whole idea was still a struggle for me, but it was obvious he was serious with this new idea. Within a month of acquiring our new project, we found out we were having another baby. Naturally, I was exhausted, but we already signed onto this major project. There was no backing out. *What the heck were we thinking?*

For the most part, it was his project, although I tried to help in between schoolwork and taking care of our children's needs. There were many days spent with a paint brush in my hand, while trying to entertain the kids just to have some family time. We ripped carpet up, and even knocked down walls. While he worked on the inside of the house, my time was spent working on landscaping and the kids ran back and forth for attention. The days were long, and the projects seemed endless. Most evenings, he stayed late to work, while I left with Grace and Jack to maintain their bedtime routines.

Family meals were important to me, so dinner was something I put together most nights. If time allowed, we would even have dessert. Knowing my husband's schedule and commute, family dinner was ready by six o'clock. There were so many evenings of fighting tears, when six o'clock would come, six-thirty, and sometimes seven o'clock, and my husband still wasn't home. Even the kids would get crabby and tired from the wait. *Where was he? How can his commute take this long?*

It was easy to get a little resentful, knowing the amount of time and effort being poured into making sure, with minimal success, we had family time. There was finally a breaking point where family dinner was at six o'clock, with or without my husband. And many nights, the kids and I ate together without their father. His arrival was often during my time of juggling the children's needs and cleaning up after dinner. Even then, he would eat for ten minutes, play with the kids for thirty minutes, and then he was off to the remodel project until late evening, and sometimes early morning hours.

This "quick" six-week remodel literally took over months of our marriage, as it dictated our evenings and weekends. By this time, we both had full time careers, so the only family time we had was evenings and weekends. Days turned into months. To say I was missing my husband was a complete understatement. At this point, I was also feeling completely alone and exhausted from my pregnancy, taking care of our children...not to mention still juggling college homework.

Desperate for his attention, I literally begged for "couple" time with him—not as his painter, landscaper, or nanny. It was obviously time for a real date, with real conversation about anything other than a house remodel or kids' schedules. We needed to get our marriage back on track; it was crumbling.

One evening, while he was working late on the house, I called him and asked him when he had some time available to take me on a date. That conversation brought on tears, with me pouring my heart out to him about feeling empty and needing some time with him soon. We agreed to me finding a sitter for the children and us going to dinner the following Saturday evening.

All week long, the only thing on my mind was finally being able to spend an evening with my husband. Dinner was planned out, and a sitter was arranged to come watch the kids. My clothes were picked out, which were limited by my being nearly eight months pregnant. It felt good to be able to finally have some quality time with my husband.

Saturday finally arrived. Earlier in the week, we agreed that he would work at the remodel house most of the day, and then come home at four o'clock to get ready to leave for dinner. My day was spent getting the house in order and preparing dinner for the babysitter.

Late afternoon arrived, and I started getting ready for our date night. My hair was all fixed up and my make-up was glowing. And even though my clothes were ready for the date, my outfit was changed several times in trying to find something that made me look my best with a large pregnant belly.

Four o'clock had finally arrived. The kids and I were playing while we watched and waited for their father's arrival. Fifteen minutes passed by and he still hadn't arrived, which wasn't unusual as he was always late. Thirty minutes passed. Since the sitter was due to arrive by five o'clock, it seemed necessary to call him.

The phone call involved him explaining how time had gotten away, as he ran into a huge problem on the house. He apologized, saying he couldn't just leave it, but thought he would have it ironed out within the hour. With the plans getting changed, the sitter was contacted, and her scheduled arrival time was pushed to six o'clock, hoping that would give my husband plenty of time to fix whatever needed to be fixed. His timeline seemed sketchy given the 20-minute commute, but I had no choice but to trust his judgement of time.

Another hour rolled by and the scene was still the same. Again, I found myself calling my husband to find out if he was on his way, since the sitter would be arriving soon. He apologized to me again and explained that he was still tied up on this massive project. He was unable to give me an exact time but hoped it would only be another hour or so. With that information, it was obviously time to cancel the babysitter. *What a waste of a time.*

All week long, I had been looking forward to a date with my husband. That evening was much needed for the sanity of our marriage. Instead, my time was spent eating dinner with the kids without my husband, like usual, trying to hold it together for the children. Once they went to bed, the flood of tears poured out.

My husband did arrive home within a couple of hours, but by that time, we were without a sitter and I was too exhausted and emotionally drained to go anywhere. And even though he was apologetic, it was obvious he had no idea what that night meant to me. That was honestly the start of me looking at him much differently.

Over the next few weeks, my attempts to arrange quality time would get dismissed. He gave me a list of things that needed to get done, and with that, he couldn't commit to a time to spend with me. Attempts at trying to get him to agree to just a couple of hours together, would only result in him reminding me of how behind he was on getting the house done, and he couldn't break away.

In his long list of projects, he mentioned mowing the lawn. *I can mow the lawn.* Thinking it would take something off of his lengthy list, my plan was to tackle the task, hoping it would free up some of his time for me.

The kids picked out some stuff to play with and we left to go meet their father at the project house. After getting the kids set up, I fired up the mower and mowed the lawn. The neighbors were most likely entertained watching me waddle through the yard, nearly nine months pregnant, but that didn't bother me. After finishing up, nearly forty-five minutes later, and feeling proud, I asked if he could join us for dinner now that he had the extra time. Nope. Dinner would consist of me fighting back tears while entertaining the children. *I hated this house.*

As time went on, the man that came to my bed late at night was a complete stranger. We barely shared words with each other in the mornings or evenings. Often times, his dinner was left in the microwave for him, as the kids and I moved on with our evening routine. The resentment developed to full force, as I watched my husband care more about everything and everyone else, than for me or my needs. My marital bank was completely bankrupted. It was easier to avoid him, than to lash out my frustrations at him in front of our children.

The birth of Luci was scheduled for induction, which was an exciting day. It was also the most time my husband and I had been together in months. Even through that exciting day, he was on his phone and laptop most of the day. He spent his time writing haikus, and texting updates to everyone about our moment-by-moment progress, which completely annoyed me.

After Luci arrived, we were so focused on the miracle of her and the bonding between the children that we sort of forgot about the state of our marriage. We were flooded with visitors and family, which didn't leave room to think about much else.

There was a brief high after we brought Luci home, as we learned to care for our family together. My husband was actually committed to helping at home that first week, acknowledging my limited abilities after just giving birth. Honestly, his help was needed and appreciated with the new transition of our family. We were actually having conversations together, enjoying meals together as a family, and putting the kids to bed together at night. It was starting to feel like we had passed the trying times.

Unfortunately, it wasn't long before the old routine set back in, and I was back to being a single, lonely mother. Only this time, there was another person—a new baby—depending on me. Days turned into months. Months turned into half of a year, before I hit my breaking moment, which in all reality, was already too late. By this point, feeling completely lonely, my desire to keep our marriage together was completely gone.

In thinking about our family, came demands for us to attend marriage counseling. It did seem to help at times, as my frustrations were vented, but it still felt like his heart wasn't with me anymore. He was often late to the therapy sessions, sometimes arriving over halfway through the session. *Does he even care about our marriage? Does he even care about me anymore?*

At one of our sessions, it was recommended by the therapist that we fill out a notecard with five things we wanted from each other. We were instructed to exchange the notecard and take the next thirty days to fulfill each other's requests, spreading out the tasks as a way to re-connect. In understanding my need for acts of service, this assignment was exciting, as it forced him to show his appreciation for me through actions, and not just his words.

The next couple of days were utilized to carefully plan the ways for me to carry out his requests. I chose one day each week to achieve his desired requests, putting a lot of thought and time into each. Over a two-day period, at the end of the deadline, he gave me all five of my notated requests. This was a realization that our marriage was coming to an end.

A month later, my uncle Ray called to see how my family and I were doing. Over the years, we tried to catch up with each other every six months or so. He was just eighteen years older than me, soaking up a successful career as a pharmacist in a large city a few hours away. As we talked about our families, he broke the news to me about how he had just moved into an apartment, as he and my aunt had decided to separate a few months prior and were continuing with a divorce.

This was shocking news to hear, and I found myself pouring out my own frustrations and marital unhappiness. He listened and gave me his thoughts on my stress as well as some words of encouragement. As we hung up the phone, he said, "Remember, life is too short. No matter what you decide to do for your family, find your happiness."

A couple of months later, while standing in my kitchen to clean up after breakfast, my adoptive mother called me to tell me that my uncle Ray, her brother, had passed away unexpectedly. Hearing this devastating news was so heartbreaking, especially since we had just visited on the phone a couple of months prior. He was only 47 years-old; he was so healthy! *If I only get 18 more years to live my life, is this how it should be spent?*

A few days later, we were attending his mass burial. While standing in front of the church, preparing for my reading, I kept glancing over at my husband. He was sitting next to our three children, looking at me smiling. While reading through the scripture and glancing at my husband, it occurred to me that my time could be just as short as my uncle's time had been.

Even though it appeared his full attention was finally on me, the feeling of emptiness was real. Thinking about what my uncle's last words were to me a month prior, I knew I needed to find my happiness and not take life for granted. His last words kept echoing in my mind. *This is not what my children should think a marriage is: two people that are just there, feeling forced to stay despite being miserable.*

Over the next couple of days, my thoughts were more and more focused on the need to proceed with dissolving our marriage, and not forcing a relationship that felt one-sided. Those same thoughts were shared with our marriage therapist the following week while we were waiting for my husband to attend. She said she could see my frustrations, as well as the lost hope for our marriage, and felt we needed to discuss these serious thoughts with my husband.

Well, we were not able to discuss my anxieties during that session, because he was more than thirty minutes late. Unfortunately, that was becoming a common occurrence with him, which even the therapist pointed out. Nearly each time he was late, sometimes 30 – 45 minutes late. He justified it by acknowledging he just couldn't get away.

Why did he even bother? It seemed like it simply wasn't that important to him, because if it were actually a priority, he would make the time rather than making excuses.

More resentment built up, which prompted me to ask him to move out, as we needed some time apart. That was the hardest thing to have to do. It needed to happen so I could know for sure if my overwhelming feelings were genuine. Perhaps the time apart would get his attention, and maybe he would put more focus on our marriage, and honestly, our family.

The next few days were tough. Being alone with the children wasn't anything out of the ordinary as it felt like I was a single mother for the most part already. In all honesty, it didn't really feel like much had changed at all, except that eerie feeling waking up in the night to a lonely bed. Within a few days, we sat down to go through a shared child custody schedule, and then reality hit at the realization of planning lonely evenings.

We divided our time equally with the children, as part of our shared custody arrangement. My new quiet home, without my children needing me, was agonizing. This new feeling was beyond depressing and lonely. There were times when my children's voices were heard at night even though they were not actually there. This only confirmed my heart was breaking. All the times I'd wished for just a few minutes to myself now haunted me. My evenings were honestly too quiet. *Was this really my new life?*

Ingredient
Faith

Often associated with the Virgin Mary, the lemon is a symbol of fidelity in love.

WE ENDED UP KICKING OUR RENTERS OUT OF THE HOUSE THAT MY HUSBAND HAD JUST RENOVATED, SO THAT HE COULD LIVE THERE. THAT FIRST NIGHT, DROPPING the KIDS OFF TO MY SOON-TO-BE EX-HUSBAND, IN HIS OWN HOME, WAS BRUTAL. THE ENTIRE TEN-MINUTE DRIVE HOME, after so much anxiety from dropping them off, WAS FILLED WITH ME SOBBING. ONCE I arrived HOME, THERE WERE MORE TEARS as I realized MY HOME WAS EMPTY, AND NOT A FAMILY HOME. OVER THE NEXT FEW WEEKS, MY TEARS WERE CONSTANT, AND AT TIMES UNCONTROLLABLE.

Even though it was incredibly difficult, my secret pain was concealed in front of the children. Many nights ended with me crying myself to sleep. The struggles in my personal life were masked even to those closest to me, mostly because of embarrassment, but also because I didn't want any sympathy about the situation.

Even though it was for the best, it was still a tough realization that our marriage was over. *How could 11 years have shifted into a completely different life for us? How could it be that we fell out of love with each other? Where did we lose the drive we had for our marriage? For each other? He was once my crush. How did we get to this place?*

So many thoughts poured through my mind for weeks thinking about all the years we shared together. Eleven years of new friendships, weddings, funerals, babies, careers, college, and yet, somehow along the way, we failed to put each other's needs first. It seemed like I was the one putting forth all of the effort, yet not receiving a lot in return. Somewhere we stopped being a couple. We didn't go on dates or share time together like we had for years. We got so wrapped up in being a mother and father, and focused on our own personal wants, that we forgot how to need each other.

As the weeks went by, I was smiling on the outside, but the reality was that I was a complete mess with accepting the reality of it all. One day, while going through some stuff in my closet, Grace brought me this little prayer card. She said, "Mom, look what I found on my closet floor." In a quick glance at what she had in her hand, it looked like a bookmark, which was quickly shrugged off.

Later, after Grace had gone to bed, that object caught my eye. In studying it, I realized it was not a bookmark, rather a prayer card. And not just any prayer card, but a prayer card for St. Theresa. In reading the back of the small card, the message was profound.

It read,

May today there be peace within.

May you trust you are exactly where you are meant to be.

May you not forget the infinite possibilities that are born of faith in yourself and others.

May you use the gifts that you have received, and pass on the love that has been given to you.

May you be content with yourself just the way you are.

Let this knowledge settle into your bones, and allow your soul the freedom to sing, dance, praise, and love.

It is there for each and every one of us.

Where on earth had Grace found this? Chills covered my arms. The message from that prayer card was so relevant to my personal feelings. Just how did Grace come up with this prayer card? In exploring her closet, it was unclear of where Grace found the card. When walking out of her closet, I noticed she was still awake, so we chatted about the card she brought me. She told me of how she walked into her closet and it was laying on the floor.

With this explanation, she led me to the spot in her closet, on the floor, where she found the card. In looking at the top of her closet shelf at her baptism box, a quick memory came to mind of her receiving a prayer card at her baptism. Since I didn't have many mementos from my childhood, it was important for me to cherish such wonderful memories when possible. With further observation, there was no way she could have reached the box that held those memories. *How on earth did that get on the floor?*

A few days later, I was visiting with my two neighbors who also happened to be Catholic nuns. I shared with them the story about Grace bringing me the prayer card. Through our conversation, I explained how her discovery didn't make any sense, as it wasn't possible for her to reach the area where that card was stored. One of the nuns explained, "Perhaps, it was a message from God, as if whispering into Grace's ear, 'Go, take this to your mother.'" This thought hadn't occurred to me before, but after looking further into her closet, there wasn't any other reasonable explanation.

That day, my faith had been restored. Regardless of how that card got to Grace, and then to me, it became my reliance. That card remained by my bedside and was read nearly every night. After reading it, I prayed and asked for help during my lonely time, and it wasn't long before that faith carried me to a new beginning.

Through my new faith, came the realization of the root of my newfound anxiety. My anxiety was due to my routine being so different, and the struggle of trying to establish a new routine through a different perspective. Sure, being without my children was brutal, but the reality was that a new routine was desperately needed to keep me positive and sane.

Whenever my new situation gave me doubts, I remembered that a new routine is what I needed. Otherwise my mind would wonder about all of those, "what ifs." I had been plagued by those before and they were unproductive. *Tomorrow is a new day!*

A new day meant a new gym membership. My quiet evenings were replaced with exercise and friendships, as I arranged to meet my friends at the gym after work. No more quiet evenings of tears and anxiety. By the time my workouts ended in the evenings, it was nearly time for bed.

Over the course of the next few months, my kids' father and I sat down, amicably, and worked through our divorce, including our child custody schedule, which was necessary for a court record. He protested the divorce and refused to attend the final court hearing. My gut told me to follow my heart and stick to what was best for my children —even it wasn't what was in my original fantasies for what my family would be.

Ultimately, my kid's father and I both realized that we would be happier apart than forcing an obligation on ourselves for the sake of our children. Through the months ahead, our routines got easier, and our faith in our ability to co-parent got easier.

Bad Lemon 6
Toxic Environment

In European tradition, the lemon is a symbol of fidelity and wealth.

A COUPLE OF MONTHS after my divorce, while sitting in my car at the bank drive thru and waiting for the tellers to process a transaction, I overheard the tellers having a conversation. It was obvious they didn't realize they had left the microphone on. "You know that is the ex-wife of our old controller..." The small-town gossip completely annoyed me.

The teller, smiling, gave me my transaction slip and wished me a good day, as if that entire conversation hadn't been heard. It generally takes a lot to get me fired up, but that sent me over the edge. After pulling my car out of the drive-thru lane and straight into a parking stall, I gathered the children out of the car, and then marched straight into the bank.

After a quick discussion with one of the bank vice presidents, about the need to close out my account, one of the tellers looked over at me, recognized her wrongdoing, and apologized to me. While trying to keep myself in check in front of the children, I reminded them that my children who were in the backseat heard them gossiping, which was completely unprofessional. Thankfully, the kids hadn't actually heard a thing, but that wasn't the point.

That was the first time after my divorce, that I witnessed negative things being said about me and my failed marriage. Unfortunately, that was honestly just the beginning. From that point on, any discussion about my divorce was muted. Whenever someone would ask how my children's father was – to which, their sincerity was questionable in my mind -- their question would get dismissed with, "He's great." Anything to shut down the conversation.

Even when someone would ask me how I was doing; their sincerity was questioned. *Do you really want to know or are you just being nosey?* Often, their questions would get dismissed with, "I'm doing great. And you?" Which was often followed by, "I heard about your divorce. I am so sorry to hear about it. What happened?" *Are you kidding me?*

Why did something have to happen? Was there something written on my face that made it appear is if my personal business was open for discussion? And why did people feel it was even appropriate to even ask me about it? Though annoyed, each question was followed by some positive way of shutting down the entire conversation. "We just grew apart, and realized we were better off separate than together." That explanation most often resulted in some big eyes and fake smiles, which was obviously not an acceptable answer to the wondering minds. They wanted real gossip and juicy information to be able to repeat to others in our small town.

During that first year after my divorce, there were challenges with trying to juggle friendships, family and even being a working single mother. Dealing with a divorce in a small community was difficult enough but finding a healthy balance to appreciate my new chapter was essential. It wasn't a secret that it was a struggle in finding that balance. In reflecting back throughout that year, the relationships around me were dictating my mood.

A few weeks post-divorce, one of my sister's mother asked me one day, "How are you affording your house now that you're divorced?" *Wow.* It appeared the real concern was about my finances, and not really my well-being. Later, a couple of friends would tell me about how she was telling them my divorce was due to the extra marital affairs that both of us were having. *Honestly, what the hell?*

After hearing such ridiculous gossip, it was obvious we needed to discuss the need for her to respect my privacy. She fully admitted the inappropriate conversations she had and justified her actions because we wouldn't tell her why we were choosing to divorce. *Why did I need to explain my choices, as an adult, to her?* Irritated by the lack of respect, I reminded her that it didn't give her the right to make up stuff, and how her gossip sounded credible, given that everyone knew she was my mother. My trusted circle began getting smaller.

During that same time, one of my sister's was experiencing a loss of her own, as her best friend's sister was brutally killed. After hearing the news, it seemed appropriate to offer my condolences to my sister, as well as my offer to help with anything she needed. A couple of days later, out of respect for my grieving sister and her friend, I made an effort to attend the visitation to offer my condolences. Later that evening, my sister sent me a text asking me to call her.

There was obviously no way to prepare for what was about to unfold. As she answered my call, her tone sounded completely disgusted with me as she questioned my attendance at the visitation of her best friend's sister. Remaining silent, I let her vent and belittle me, "Why were you at the visitation tonight? You didn't even know her?"

The tone of her voice, as well as her obvious anger, were both baffling to me, but at the same time, I considered the stress and grief she was feeling. "To pay my respects to her family and to support you." My response to her questions obviously wasn't what she wanted to hear as she was so angry with me. She then told me that she didn't think my presence was warranted, especially since I didn't actually know her best friend's sister.

It was incredibly difficult for me to understand why she was so upset at my way of showing her respect. Why did there have to be a reason to attend a visitation? Her best friend spent many days and nights at our house growing up, so it most definitely seemed appropriate to extend my condolences to her as well. Seriously, why would she question my respect for her? More importantly, why did there need to be ANY excuse to show my support for her?

This whole ridiculous situation made me wonder if my sister had issues with funerals, remembering how silly she was when our biological father passed away a couple of years earlier. After he died, we agreed to meet at the funeral since it was six hours away. Meanwhile, my father-in-law and mother-in-law, along with my brother-in-law and his wife, had made arrangements to make the drive to support me and pay their respects.

Following our birth father's funeral, my sister cornered me, and asked me, "Why are your in-laws here?"

Looking at her, puzzled by her actually questioning their presence, I answered, "To pay their respects and support me." She quickly replied, "But they didn't even know our dad." *You are absolutely right! That is why one attends funerals is to make sure the deceased knows they were there. You have to be kidding.* Despite being so completely annoyed with her level of thinking, I still found a tasteful way to end the useless conversation.

And so, here we were again, focusing more negative energy surrounding a funeral, as if I was some kind of funeral whore. *Christ! Who honestly enjoys attending funerals?* In efforts to end the useless conversation and her questioning my intentions, it was mutually agreed for me to skip the funeral.

That evening was filled with a lot of tears, at the realization of the dynamic of our sisterly relationship. It just felt like I was constantly walking on eggshells around her. When having conversations with her, my words were often chosen carefully, so that she didn't get upset with me. Many times, conversations were awkward in efforts to avoid her getting offended or her taking my comments in the wrong way.

We had gone through so much together since our childhood, yet it was a harsh reality of who cared more about keeping a relationship. In all honesty, it was a relationship that served no purpose, as it often just fostered stress and emotions that simply were not warranted. With age, the black cloud of constant negative energy became more and more exhausting.

There was no question that there was genuine love for her, but the constant apologizing for stuff that never made sense was becoming too much for my mind and heart. At the end of the day, having a desirable relationship was not reciprocated, and was literally sucking the life out of me. The tears flooded my face through the night when trying to make sense of it all. *Maybe it is time to let go of trying to force what isn't there.*

My children's father and I had a good co-parenting relationship post-divorce, as we both had the same vested interest: our children's happiness. We tried to have dinners together with the kids, as well as do family things together when our schedules allowed. We even celebrated the children's birthdays together, which was often questioned. Was there an unwritten rule saying that you have to hate your ex?

One hot summer day, the kiddos wanted to go to the swimming pool. At the time, Grace was seven years old, Jack was four years old, and Luci was a year old. As anyone could imagine, taking three kids to a public pool, none of whom knew how to swim, was most definitely a challenge. Grace liked going down the slides, Jack was busy in the water, and Luci enjoyed the splash area, which basically meant we covered all bases of the public pool. Thankfully, their father agreed to meet us there to help manage the fun.

My children's father and I were taking turns with Luci when one of my sister's mom and aunt walked into the pool area. After greeting them, we chatted for a few minutes before finding my way to my children to re-apply their sunscreen. While rubbing the kids down with sunscreen, it was obvious by their body language that my sister's mother and aunt were talking about me and my children's father. Their constant stares as we managed our children quickly got annoying, so it was time to go chat with them.

They were sitting in the zero-entry section of the pool, so I made my way over there and sat down next to them. The first thing one of them said to me, "Why is he here?" Completely annoyed with her questioning our need to continue a healthy co-parenting relationship, I replied, "He's my kids' father. Why wouldn't he be here?" She responded, "I just think it's very weird that you two are here, at the pool hanging out like nothing is wrong."

While completely irritated with her judgment, I blurted out my response, "I didn't realize there was something wrong. So, honestly, what is wrong?"

It was difficult to carry on at the pool, as if the level of selfish judging was not affecting me. Unfortunately, the more the conversation replayed in my mind, it did bother me. *Why do I have to justify what is right for my children to them?* Thankfully, the kids were worn out, so we packed up and made our way out of the pool.

Fast forward another eighteen months, and the dynamic of my children's father and my relationship drastically shifted. While we promised to always put the children's needs first, we failed to understand how that would actually work once we both developed relationships with significant others. The growing hostility resorted to novel emotional email exchanges, and eventually utilizing the police for our custody handoffs.

There were so many sleepless nights of anxiety and tears in realizing my life was spinning out of control. There appeared to be so much toxicity all around me. Each new day was tackled by plugging away at my career and the focus of being the best mother in the moment. From the outside, the overwhelming stress was masked with a fake smile. I desperately needed a change of pace.

One evening, while visiting with my son, I observed how negative he was about everything. It seemed he needed to project his complaints, which was probably what he was witnessing from me. Thinking my stress was hidden from the children, the reality was just the opposite. My demeanor was projecting my negativity and stress, without me actually realizing it.

During the past eighteen months of going through a separation, and then a divorce, I thought I was holding it together and shielding my children from my actual pain. Unfortunately, the truth was blatantly obvious as now my son was mimicking what he had been seeing from his own mother. *My kids do not deserve this.* That was it for me. It was time to stop setting my children up for failure through my own catastrophe.

In that conversation with my son, his complaints were stopped by asking him to tell me five positive things about his day. It was a struggle to pull out five things at first, but he was able to tell me about a funny moment at lunch, followed by acing his spelling test, and then bragging about pushing some girls on the swings at recess. Holy success!

Now it was my turn to recognize my own positive environment, which clearly, I had lost sight of somehow. That evening was spent making a list of all the positive things in my life. My health was great. Not only was I blessed with amazing children, but they were also healthy. My career afforded me reliable transportation, as well as a beautiful home to share with my children. My healthy, reliable friendships consisted of the same friends since middle school, high school, and volunteering. God was looking out for me. Anything outside of those attributes, simply were not worth wasting any more energy on.

Ingredient
Detoxing and Keeping My Glass Half Full

Lemons represent honesty, redemption and internal cleansing and are often used to cleanse your soul, body, and mind.

AFTER ACKNOWLEDGING ALL MY reasons to be grateful, I began formulating a plan to continue to surround myself with positive energy. It was time to stop reacting to unwanted opinions, remove individuals from my life who created tension and stress, and find a way to communicate with my kids' father that didn't result in hostility. Lastly, I needed to model positive behavior for the success of my children's future.

Hearing lies and opinions about me from others was such a struggle for me. Honestly, why did my actions have to be justified to anyone? Why did it matter what others thought about me? All that mattered was the truth. It also occurred to me that people hear what they want to hear and see what they want to see, and fair or not, repeat that information accordingly. I thought about all of the times I heard gossip and then judged that person without knowing what had actually happened firsthand. *What was wrong with me? Who was I to judge?*

Acknowledging there are three sides to every story, I felt like such a fool to have others' words dictate my opinions for so many years. A great example is the "bank incident." Regardless of what certain ladies had heard, they obviously heard inaccurate information, yet they believed it. The truth is honestly difficult to know for certain, because it is clouded by perception: my kids' father's perspective, mine, and the truth lying somewhere in between.

Making any judgement based off of hearsay is simply a waste of time. This new thought forced me to realize that others were just reacting to what they had heard. From that point on, there was no more entertainment of any opinion that didn't affect someone in my house. When hearing gossip, my simple reply was, "If it doesn't impact someone at 257 (my house number), I honestly do not care."

I thought even further about all of the assumptions I made based on my own perception of what was seen. For example, seeing an old friend in a grocery store and asking if the man with her was her husband, only to realize that the man was actually her brother. Or the time I saw a sales associate in Home Depot who looked pregnant, only to find out after asking when her baby was due, that she actually had a baby four months prior. And the number of times my oldest two children get questioned about how long they have been dating when they go out together is baffling. All of these thoughts only prove that people see what they want to see.

In my pursuit to channel positive energy around me, I began evaluating my relationships and friendships. A colleague once told me that friendships and relationships should always be about building success for each other. In addition, having trusting relationships and encouragement are part of helping to build success. If at any point any one of those attributes are violated, then those relationships are toxic. *Ouch!* Of course, being cordial was ideal, but beyond that, those individuals didn't deserve my attention.

With that, it was easy to weed out individuals who surrounded me with negative energy. With heartache, I realized my sister was included. Making the decision to distance myself from her was difficult and brought on a flood of tears. The reality was, those tears were really about letting go of all that we had been through together over the years; because outside of those experiences, the relationship was obviously toxic.

The fear of losing our childhood bond ultimately created more risk than any benefit. It was true, we had gone through a lot together during our childhood, but my focus needed to be on my own family and not babysitting her emotions and mood swings.

It is clear that my choice proved to be accurate. The relationship died as soon as my efforts ended. It opened my eyes to seeing just how one-sided everything had been all along, because if she genuinely cared, then she would have made the effort to check in on me. My phone did not ring.

In respecting the choice to let my sister live her life, it was also time to separate myself from her source of reliance: her adoptive family. Their generosity will always be appreciated; however, the reality was that they chose her to be in their family when they chose to adopt her as a child. They were only helping out their new daughter's biological sister in a time of need. My sister needed them, and it was not my place to take that away from her, especially when maintaining that relationship would have created stress for me anyway.

As difficult as it was, it was time to remove myself from all of her family, out of respect for their relationship with my sister. My sister will forever hold a special place in my heart, but it was a time in life for us to focus on our children. Despite all the unnecessary heartache, I will continually wish the best for her and her family. I will always love her and cherish the strength she gave me during our childhood.

The same thing applied for other unhealthy friendships that honestly served no purpose. It was time to stop running in circles to ensure everyone around me was happy—and find my own happiness. Once my focus shifted away from worthless friendships to low-maintenance friendships, my happiness began to blossom.

My kids' father and I also found a healthy place for a positive co-parenting relationship. Thankfully, we both once again recognized that we had the same vested interest: our children and their happiness. Obviously, if we agreed on everything, we would still be married. We both vowed to focus on the safety, education, and overall health of our children. Anything outside of that was fueled by our personal emotions, which didn't matter.

Sure, there were still frustrating situations; however, no amount of anger or hatred would ever outweigh my love for our children. My children's father and I were now dedicated to operating our co-parenting relationship much like running a business, by removing all emotions and personal opinions. Ensuring a successful future for our children was contingent upon our ability to make positive and professional exchanges.

Surrounding myself with positive relationships that kept my glass half full also made me a better mother, as there was minimal stress to release around them. They deserved nothing less than a positive and healthy environment.

Bad Lemon 7
Facing My Genealogy

She had known happiness, exquisite happiness, intense happiness, and it silvered the rough waves a little more brightly, as daylight faded, and the blue went out of the sea and it rolled in waves of pure lemon which curved and swelled and broke upon the beach and the ecstasy burst in her eyes and waves of pure delight raced over the floor of her mind and she felt, It is enough! It is enough!

Virginia Woolf (Adeline Virginia Stephen)
English writer. (1882——1941)

SINCE MY EIGHTEENTH birthday, it was a priority for me to see a gynecologist annually. Somewhere in my younger years, I had been told that my biological grandmother had died in her early forties, from ovarian cancer or cancer of the uterus; it really wasn't known for sure since autopsies were not advanced in 1971. Having limited knowledge of my family history, it was important for me to be proactive with any and all routine appointments.

Around my twenty-sixth birthday, my children's father and I were wrestling with the idea of having another baby. Since my previous pregnancy resulted in a cesarean delivery, my fear was that any future pregnancies would end with a cesarean. That was an unpleasant experience for me and required a longer amount of time to heal. Going up and down stairs while holding a pillow over my stomach was awful. The idea of going through all of that again was dreadful, so the only way I would even consider having another baby was through promises of a natural delivery.

During the research process of finding doctors who would perform a vaginal birth after cesarean (VBAC), I stumbled upon my current doctor. At the initial consultation with her, her positive energy was infectious, which was easy to fall in love with. We were nearly the same age, as she was in her first months out of her doctorate program. She spoke incredibly fast and was high energy, which reminded me of myself.

At that visit, she advised that any risks or complications associated with having a VBAC was less than a five percent in my case. She quickly acknowledged that the only reason there was a need for my prior cesarean was due to complications with my son, and not due to any complications related to my ability to deliver naturally. She felt comfortable performing a VBAC, and so that day began many years of establishing a great patient/doctor relationship.

Over the years of seeing her through routine appointments and two pregnancies, we shared a lot about our families. Since we both spoke incredibly fast, we could cover a lot of conversation in a short time. In our conversations, I learned that she was a mother of two, married to a high-profile attorney, and grew up watching her nurse practitioner mother, which ultimately inspired her to go into the medical field. She had considered following in her mother's footsteps; however, she loved surgery, so she decided to become a doctor instead.

From our first visit, and throughout the years, we conversed about any potential risks associated with the possibility of cancer in my family history. Since she knew my family history was limited, she always took extra caution to address any necessary testing or ultrasounds. Knowing how serious she took my health made it easy to trust her. While most of my girlfriends despise those annual visits, I, on the other hand, actually look forward to them.

On my thirty-fifth birthday, I was at my gynecologist's office to get my annual exam done. Following the nurse back to the exam room, there stood my doctor in the hallway. She looked at me puzzled, and we exchanged a quick hug, wishing each other a happy new year. She was looking through her schedule and acknowledging that she didn't see my name as a patient for the day.

While preparing all of my annual appointments for the beginning of the year, which also happened to be my non-busy time at work, she was booked out for over four months. Waiting that long to schedule with her would have put my appointment in the busiest part of our season, so it made sense to just book with someone that was available rather than waiting so long.

She seemed disappointed, but ultimately understood my explanation. She even told me I should have left a message with the nurse to have her call me, as she would have worked me into her schedule. Of course, troubling her with working me into her busy schedule would not have been anything I would have considered. We chatted for a couple of minutes before I was led into the exam room by the nurse, where she gathered my routine vitals for the doctor.

Right as the nurse was leaving the room, my doctor peaked into the room and said, "Hey, okay, so you are my patient and I'm going to be seeing you today." To say that her persistence was a shock was honestly an understatement, but I was also grateful to be seeing her instead of a stranger. She told me the doctor I was waiting on was already behind on schedule for the day, and she didn't want me to have to wait. She instructed me to get undressed and said that she would return within a few minutes.

The seemed the first initial five-to-ten minutes of my appointments with her was always spent catching up on our families, before going through the exam process. As we visited through my exam, she told me that she really thought me having genetic testing done would be beneficial. She explained that genetic testing is performed through lab work and can detect any genetic mutations that may result in cancer. She told me as she had learned more about the testing, she had thought about me, and even thought about calling me several times to make that suggestion to me.

She further explained that the test results could help determine or even prevent any future treatments, especially if the results came back to prove that I was not at high risk for any gender specific cancer. She explained that although she loved seeing me each year, annual visits may not be necessary, especially if we could rule out any genetic mutations associated with cancer. She advised that her office would bill my insurance for the lab work, and worst-case scenario, I would receive a bill for the procedure, which was no more than $375.00. She ended her conversation by telling me that most of the time the results come back with nothing, but that she felt having the extra knowledge could greatly benefit my peace of mind.

In thinking about the possibility of knowing a piece of my genetic make-up, the decision seemed easy to make, realizing $375.00 was worth that peace of mind. We agreed to have the labs drawn before leaving her office that day. Even if it cost me a little bit, having the knowledge was definitely worth it.

Sitting there getting several vials of blood drawn, the phlebotomist told me that the results would be back in around six weeks, and my doctor would contact me with the findings. Leaving the office, it felt good knowing the concerns about being a carrier for cancer would be addressed through lab results. Hopefully, the results would prove that there wasn't a reason to be so paranoid about cancer.

Nearly three weeks after my appointment, while gathering some items in my car in preparation for a marketing meeting with a friend, my phone rang. The call was from my gynecologist and she wanted to discuss the results of my genetic testing. We sat in the car as my doctor explained that she had just gotten off the phone with the pathologist, who had read my lab results to her over the phone.

She admitted she had not seen the actual results yet; however, the pathologist was quite concerned about the findings. My test results indicated a positive result for three genetic mutations; two of which were for the exact same cancer: colon cancer. With me being in the 80-100 percent category for colon cancer, the pathologist was concerned about the report, as someone with such high numbers should have begun routine colonoscopies at least ten years earlier.

My heart was pounding so hard as I listened to her explain what little information she currently knew but would receive before the end of the day. She advised that she was going to schedule an appointment with The Cancer Research Center to have a genetic counselor go over the results with me, so that any questions about the blood test results could be quickly and confidently answered.

In addition, she advised that she had reached out to a couple of her doctor friends who specialized in gastrointestinal health, and she wanted me to schedule a colonoscopy as soon as possible. She also explained that the other genetic mutation that I tested positive for, was also linked to breast and thyroid cancer, but that further discussions with a genetic counselor could cover the details more accurately.

My friend sat through the entire conversation in my car with me. I knew she was absorbing the same information, as I could see it on her face throughout the phone call. When the call ended, she gave me a hug and tried to convince me to skip the marketing meeting. Although I was very overwhelmed after processing that phone call, I knew the best thing was for me to continue with the meeting. I quickly realized that there was really nothing I could do in that moment until I received the full genetic report, therefore, keeping busy would be better for my mental state.

That afternoon my doctor's office called me to advise that my genetic report was ready to be picked up. The entire afternoon was devoted to reading through that lengthy report in its entirety, before making appointments with The Cancer Research Center, Gastrointestinal Specialist, and Breast Specialist. Reading through the information was completely overwhelming, but I was relieved when The Cancer Research Center agreed to meet with me within a couple of days to help me better understand my test results.

Over the next few days, my mind rolled with fear. To make it worse, getting a colonoscopy wouldn't be possible for another four weeks, which really stressed me out. *What if it was too late?* Using the internet to understand more about the genetic mutations would only provide to be more stressful. Through that research, I learned that colon cancer bears minimal symptoms, which is why it is often called "the silent cancer." *What if I had cancer and didn't even know it? I have four kids who need me.*

Discovering these risks just didn't seem fair. In preparing for any possibilities, I remembered my doctor asking me about cancer insurance. With that thought on my mind, there was worry my window of opportunity might be missed, especially if all of this new information was now in my medical file. My mind was flooded with thoughts about having to pay for costly procedures. Tears from stress were flooding my face when it occurred to me to stop, breathe, and contact my insurance friend for guidance.

After sharing my results from genetic testing, and the need to have a bunch of follow up procedures, he quickly got me linked up with one of his friends who handles cancer insurance coverage. Thankfully, I was able to visit with his contact that day, and she assured me everything would be set up before there was any need for worry. Within a couple of days, that anxiety was relieved as I was fully insured for any cancer results. *Phew! What a load off!*

Within a few days, I was able to meet with a genetics counselor at The Cancer Research Center. The meeting with her offered a wealth of information as she explained the genetic report in full detail, just as my doctor had promised. She explained how my blood test results indicated I had inherited the same genetic mutation from both parents. Basically, inheriting those two genetic mutations put me in the higher probability ratio for getting cancer.

She continued to explain how those results could have easily resulted in me being the routine fifty-year-old female ending up with stage IV cancer, due to lack of genetic awareness. The bad news she delivered was that my first colonoscopy should have been performed at the age of twenty-one, and annually thereafter. She also explained that my children would need to have their first colonoscopy done by the age of twenty-five; however, genetic testing might prove that it wasn't necessary.

That meeting also gave me insight to the other genetic mutation, which was linked to both breast and thyroid cancer. Basically, my first mammogram should have been done at the age of twenty-five, as well as planning for my daughters to have theirs done at the same age. As with the potential for thyroid cancer, it was recommended that I have an ultrasound to ensure it was functioning properly. Thankfully, my thyroid had been checked a few years prior, with no concerns; however, I remembered my sisters both had issues with theirs.

As I shared that information with the genetic specialist, she advised that it would be in the best interest to give a copy of my results to both siblings right away so that they could be tested as well. She explained that both of my sisters had a fifty percent chance of inheriting the same genetic mutations, therefore they should definitely consider having genetic testing done before the age of twenty.

Leaving that appointment, I felt slightly overwhelmed, especially knowing how far behind the proactive testing was. Despite being behind, it felt good knowing my children were armored with potentially life-saving information. The only downfall was that they would need to have cancer insurance prior to any testing, and that insurance is not cheap.

Within a few weeks, all of the recommended tests had been done. Over the course of a week, my poor body had been tortured through a mammogram, a sonogram on my thyroid, and a colonoscopy. Thankfully, there were minimal concerns after getting through those appointments, and my fears of having a fatal cancer had been relieved. There were some follow up appointments and procedures, but at the end of the day, I still had the gift of tomorrow. My newfound knowledge gave me power.

Ingredient
Embracing New Family

We know our neighbors—so far as we have the right to know them. We hear of their joys and their sorrows...and hasten to make them ours so far as we may. Life in a small town is like a layer cake. One gets the whole of it, frosted top, lemon filling and all.

~ Laura Elizabeth Howe Richards
American writer. (1850 –1943)

ONCE I TURNED EIGHTEEN, I began my research to track down my biological parents. Although adoption afforded me a better lifestyle and family, for which I was grateful, there was still curiosity about my biological parents. Through the years, several memories of them came to mind, which made me wonder about them. When my birthday came each year, it was often with a thought of curiosity, wondering if they thought about me on that day. *What about Mother's Day, Father's Day, Thanksgiving and Christmas? Surely, they remembered the children they once had.*

The day my biological father and I reunited is a day that will never be forgotten. He hugged me and cried for a long five minutes. Each time I tried to break away from his tight hug, he grabbed me tighter and sobbed even more. He told me how he thought about my sisters and me daily and prayed that we were safe and doing well. When we were being adopted, he was scared of going to jail, as he knew my mother was trying to convince everyone that he did terrible stuff to us girls. He told me that was when he made the decision to move a few hours away, near my older half-sister.

He shared that he spent several sleepless nights worried about us, but believed we were in better homes with loving families. He recounted our childhood days of watching our birth mom physically abuse me and my sisters, and how he tried to protect us from her. That almost always ended in hostile fighting. He explained how heartbroken he was when he received papers requesting his signature to release us for adoption; however, he knew we would no longer be subjected to the physical abuse.

From that point on, until his death nearly seven years later, we developed a wonderful relationship. He wrote me letters almost every two weeks, and even sent presents to Grace and Jack when they were little. That melted my heart, as he lived in complete poverty and could barely afford stamps to mail a letter. Those seven years with him are years that will forever be in my heart, by getting to know the selfless, caring man that he was.

The reunion with my birth mother was the complete opposite. We decided to meet for lunch, which initially went really well. She brought gifts for the kids, and we shared a nice conversation about some of her family, which were still childhood memories for me. During a previous telephone conversation, I expressed not having many pictures from my childhood, rather only a few from my adoption book that the social worker had gathered during our adoption. She agreed to bring some pictures to our lunch meeting.

After lunch, we went outside to a picnic area and started looking through the photo albums she had brought.

We looked through two large photo albums together, as she explained the pictures, mostly of sharing holidays with my aunts, uncles, and cousins. The reunion was going really well. *This is so great! Finally, this could be the start of a great relationship, and we can all be in peace.*

That thought was amazing, until we got to the last photo album that she had brought. There we were, flipping through these beautiful pictures, of opening Christmas presents and celebrating birthdays, to pictures of a man that haunted me.

She casually kept going through the photos totally unphased by my instant stress and disgust over pictures of her boyfriend. She gloated about this wonderful man, how he was the love of her life, and THE one marriage that was meant to be. My stomach felt like it was about to explode. *Is this really happening?* In looking over at my two young children, I couldn't believe she hadn't removed those photos prior to our meeting, and still talked about him like he was a saint.

She started to explain how she was still heartbroken over his death. Her words were flowing out too freely, and she had to be stopped. Knowing my chest was about to explode, I told her there was zero desire for me to continue looking through photos of such a disgusting man. At this point, my burning chest was filled with rage, as I reminded her that he was a sick man, who violated young girls, and didn't deserve to be recognized as this "wonderful man" she sought to portray.

For the last time, she looked at me with the same cold-hearted look that once filled a room shared with a social worker. She snapped at my remarks and told me my hatefulness was a disappointment, as he really was a compassionate man. In staring at her in complete shock, she proceeded to tell me of how he died of prostate cancer, and that on his death bed, he admitted to her what he had done to my sisters and me.

She started to tear up, and her voice trembled as she continued to explain about how she had believed him over their years together, as he denied what he had done to us. She explained to me how she forgave him that day, since she knew it took a lot of courage for him to admit what he had done before he died. There she was, justifying his actions by a deathbed confession, yet I was honestly so floored by listening to her rave about a child predator. *She's not mentally stable! What mother would ever believe such crap?*

She just kept speaking, and even though her mouth was moving, my mind had lost all comprehension for what she was saying. *How could she sit there and try to convince me that he was this wonderful man? He nearly destroyed my life!* In looking at my beautiful children, carefree, playing with their father, it was obvious this meeting was a bad idea. It was time to shut her up and get the hell out of there.

There was barely an exchange of good-byes as we packed up the kids to leave. That car ride was filled with tears. I was disgusted with myself for believing there was ever a chance for a future relationship with my birth mother. That's honestly all she will ever be to me—someone who gave me life.

That meeting was the last time we spoke to each other, and for me, that decision brought me peace. The meeting proved how mentally ill she truly is. There is no way I could ever look at a situation like that with my own children and attempt to justify something so selfish and sickening. As a mother, my need to protect them would probably get me jail time before any sort of justification for inappropriate behavior that threatened their well-being.

After completing all of the medical appointments, prompted from the genetic testing, it was time to pass the fresh information off to my sisters. Since my relationship with both of my sisters was distant at the time, it was difficult to think about how to give them potentially dreadful news. There was a sense of obligation to pass on what genetic information I had discovered, so that they could get tested if they chose to. Ultimately, giving them the necessary information relieved me from having guilt should one of them end up with something that could have been prevented.

It was decided that the best way to distribute the information was to make copies of my genetic testing, and hand it off to both of them. The next day, I dropped a copy of the genetic testing off to one sister and then sent a Facebook message to my other sister with a copy as well. It was later revealed that one of my sisters had the same testing done, and thankfully, her results came back with no genetic mutations. My other sister wasn't sure that she wanted to go through with the testing, which was her choice, but I had done what I felt I needed to do.

When thinking about my family history one day, I realized there was a need to know more, especially for my children. After going through the genetic testing process, the whole process sparked a new interest. With this newfound fascination, began a new research project to track down my biological mother's siblings. I wanted to know more about my family history but lacked any desire to have a relationship with my biological mother—nor did I want her to know anything about my life or whereabouts. The whole idea was only a thought for a few weeks, before finally getting the courage to make the call.

My first call was to my biological aunt, who seemed excited to speak to me once she realized who I was. She told me how she had wondered what happened to me and my sisters and prayed that we were living happy and healthy lives. We talked about the genetic testing results, and how it prompted me to learn more about my family history, with respect to any medical issues.

We discussed what knowledge I had about my biological grandmother, her mother, and how it was understood that she died of ovarian cancer. She told me that her mother did die in the early 70's from cancer, but that it was never confirmed as to what type. She said the doctors knew that she had cancer below her naval, but couldn't pinpoint which organ actually held the cancer, especially since testing was limited back then.

Through that conversation with my aunt, she described her days as a biology professor before retirement. It was obvious her career justified her knowledge with respect to genetics. After our discussion about my genetic blood test results, we both concluded that my biological grandmother most likely died from colon cancer, and not of ovarian cancer. She also confirmed that there had been other family members with colon-related issues as well.

That day was the beginning days of having an amazing aunt, which was gratifying since my family was so small by that point. Being able to discuss my family history was an asset. Over the next few months, there were many conversations with my other aunts and uncles. Through these discussions, I learned that my biological mother was the baby of five children and was only 13 years-old when my grandmother died. There was also a large age gap between her and my aunt, therefore that created some distance.

I explained to my aunt that I respected any relationship she had with my biological mother; however, I did not want any details about me shared with her. I was relieved when she told me that my biological mother had been estranged from the rest of the family for many years. The last time she had actually seen my biological mother was at my grandfather's funeral, which had been more than sixteen years ago.

When I learned that my biological mother was only 13 years old when her own mother died, I wondered if that was why she was so disconnected from maternal instincts. Perhaps that was why she could choose a man over her children. Maybe she felt abandoned, and that's why she could easily abandon her own children.

The phone and Facebook conversations continued for almost a year before we planned to meet face-to-face. Since they lived nearly four hours away, it seemed easier for me to travel to them. One of my aunts offered for me to stay with her for that weekend, so I decided to just go for it. The thought of meeting my biological family was so incredibly exciting, yet at the same time it was very overwhelming. *What if they don't like me?*

Throughout my entire drive there, I thought about how they would react to seeing me for the first time in over thirty-five years. Sure, there were memories of them from my childhood, and also a couple of pictures in my adoption book, but that was really it.

Literally ten minutes away from my aunt's house, I called my aunt to let her know about my approximate arrival time. She told me that she had invited my other aunts and uncles to join us for dinner, as they wanted to see me again. My chest nearly exploded with excitement; her thoughtfulness to include other family members for the reunion was so incredibly sweet. Within minutes of my arrival, my uncle met me outside and literally hugged me for a few minutes.

That evening we enjoyed a nice dinner and exchanged stories. It was interesting to share some of my childhood memories, describing the scenery of family gatherings or what events we were celebrating, all the while trying to piece it all together. They shared stories about me as a baby and what they remembered about my childhood. Sitting there with this amazing family truly warmed my heart; I could feel the genuine love they still had despite the decades of unknowns. Even though my biological mother had abandoned me, it was obvious the rest of the family had carried me in their hearts through all the years.

As mentioned in a previous chapter, there are signs that lead to a specific direction. Somehow, on the day of my appointment with a new doctor, it just so happened that my actual doctor would be standing in the hallway, on my way to the exam room. That quick discussion led to her working me into her busy schedule, which prompted our conversation about getting genetic testing done. The results of those tests led me to desire more knowledge from my biological family. Not only did my doctor save my life that day, but she also brought new life to me through my amazing long-lost family.

Bad Lemon 8
Buried Potential

Praying is another way of singing.
You plant in the tree the soul of lemons.
You plant in the gardens the spirit of roses.

~ Dannie Abse
A Welsh poet and physician. 1923-2014

AFTER MY DIVORCE, VOLUNTEER work became a way for me to fill my time. Some of the volunteer work was for a local young professionals' organization, as well as the Women's Chamber and a Rotary International Club. Don't ask me how there was extra time in my busy schedule between a full-time career and managing three children, but it was difficult to say no. It didn't take long for the volunteer work to quickly pile up.

After putting in a long day of work, it was brought to my attention that I had volunteered to help with a pie tasting fundraiser at the annual Riverfest event that evening. It had totally slipped my mind. Completely exhausted from the long week, my mind was running through many reasons as a way to get out of the fundraiser. Unfortunately, guilt trumped those thoughts, and with a quick change of clothes, I made my way downtown to fulfill my commitment.

After finally finding a parking spot, it was unclear of where my assistance was needed as there were tents everywhere. In looking through my emails, it seemed easier to just call another friend who was supposed to be assisting with the same volunteer project. While making my way to the direction of the tent, there were a couple of police officers standing near the street who appeared to be there for security. One of the police officers made eye contact with me while passing by. We shared a couple of glances before I approached the tent for the pie fundraiser.

Within an hour of being there, the police officer that I shared eye contact with sauntered over to my tent. We had a few flirty exchanges before he left. Later while walking to grab something for our tent, the same officer saw me and walked straight towards me. He said, "This is going to sound like a cheesy line, but I know you from somewhere."

Remembering that we had met six months prior at a career fair, where we had discussed self-defense training, I began to laugh at his approach. "Well, it definitely IS a cheesy line, but yes, we met at the career fair a few months ago, and we discussed my friends and I doing a self-defense class that you taught." We both were laughing at this point, remembering our prior conversation. His cheesy line was the start of many dates.

Over the next few months, we spent nearly all of our free time together, which ultimately ended most of my availability for volunteer work. Within six months, we decided to integrate our two families and moved in together. By this point, my three children were three, six and nine years-old and he had one six-year-old. Our parenting styles were well established with our children. His parenting style was more directive and assertive, whereas mine was more about picking my battles with boundaries. Of course, we never really thought about how the blending process would go; we just believed it would all work out.

Despite the fact that both of us had a prior divorce, he was eager to get married again. I was skeptical. The fear of a marriage changing the dynamic of our relationship was overwhelming for me. We discussed the idea of marriage, and each time my gut told me that it wasn't for me.

After a year of dating, Jack asked me one day if he would have a stepfather. Not knowing how to respond, I asked him how he felt about it. He told me that he didn't want to be the only man of the house, but also questioned if my live-in boyfriend would move out one day, just as his father did. Not even realizing it, my children had grown attached during this trial period of my life.

In looking at my young son, I realized that it was unfair to have my children fear another potential parent leaving. Ultimately deciding to ignore my fears, I agreed to marriage—again. In my mind, I trusted that everything would work out and my relationship insecurities would go away with time. Within four months, we made our relationship official, and brought our two families together through a courthouse wedding.

The initial bliss was amazing, and everything seemed to be falling into place. We decided to exchange our two homes for a new home that accommodated our new, larger family. We settled into a new routine of getting everyone ready for the day, after school homework, family dinners and bedtime regimens. Life was moving on.

During one of my morning commutes to work, I decided to stop and grab fuel. During that stop, Kevin, one of the guys from my gym, was there. We had met a few years prior and had exchanged small talk in between switching weight machines. It was during one of those quick exchanges that he mentioned owning a lawn care business, so it seemed appropriate to ask him how the business was doing. During that visit, he told me how he was thinking about purchasing a local landscaping/plant nursery, but admitted he had no idea how to merge the two businesses.

He told me how he was scared to make the commitment, but ended our conversation by saying, "The sky is the limit." In hearing such positive words, I told him that he should pursue it. I had a passion for business operations and let him know I was happy to help if he ever needed some guidance.

A couple of weeks later, Kevin contacted me through Facebook, and asked if he could take me up on my offer in providing some feedback on his potential business purchase. He expressed concerns about taking over the nursery and wasn't sure how to assume operations; however, he did recognize that he had over 600 customers whom he thought would help grow the landscaping and nursery business. We agreed to meet later in the week to discuss everything in detail.

Over the next couple of days, I researched the nursery he was thinking about purchasing, and quickly noticed it had some bad reviews online. Furthermore, this research reminded me of my own personal experience at the same business. A few years prior, while trying to match some decorative rock, the staff was neither helpful nor friendly during my purchase. Despite what little was known about the business proposition, my mind was still flooded with a ton of ideas to pass along, which over time could easily contribute to the success of the business.

We met later in the week where I presented some ideas to him about how to merge the two businesses together. Through our conversation, we agreed it would be best for him to operate the two companies separately for at least a year. He was keeping the owners on as employees for five years, which I felt was far too long. Minimal changes upfront would allow him time to understand their operations, and to determine the best way to merge the companies into one.

He advised that winter was idle for both businesses, so it made sense to get through the first year of operations before implementing a ton of changes. Through the course of the year, he could make a list of policies, procedures, and pricing that needed to be restructured. He could then utilize the three months of his low season to implement any new ideas.

Towards the end of our meeting, it was obvious that he felt confident in his decision to move forward with the purchase. He even asked if I had any interest in becoming his business partner. I felt my efforts would be better served by helping his office manager on the side in exchange for some landscaping and lawn care maintenance.

A couple of months after that meeting, Kevin called to ask if there was time in my schedule to meet with his office manager and give her some guidance in preparation for the merge, which was scheduled to be final within sixty days. He also asked me to meet with the owners of the nursery as well, so that they could get some feedback from me on that side of the business merge. Before hanging up the phone, we agreed to meet up one night on my way home from work that following week.

Immediately walking into Kevin's office a few days later to meet his office manager, the number of stacks of handwritten invoices all over the office were completely overwhelming. *Holy moly! I bet there is easily 20 hours of handwriting in this room!*

In asking his office manager questions about their operations, it was obvious how disorganized everything was. It appeared their operations were running on the fly. We finished up our quick meeting as I jotted down some notes, and then drove down the road to the nursery to meet with the owners.

Walking in the front door, I was instantly greeted with the smell of fresh cigarettes, and a dated counter with an old cash register on it. The roll of paper on the cash register was staring at me while waiting for someone to greet me. *I truly hope they are not using that old thing!* A few minutes went by, standing at the front entrance, before I hollered out, "Hello?"

This frumpy woman walked out and said, "What do you need?" Maybe she thought my entrance involved solicitation since I was in a business suit, as she seemed completely annoyed at my existence.

Kevin had told me that through their interactions, he had told the nursery owners about me and my assistance with the merge. While introducing myself, I put out my hand to shake hers, yet she just looked down at my handshake offer and said, "What do you want?" Looking back up at her, I explained how Kevin had told me to stop in and meet with her to see if she needed any assistance in preparing for the business merge.

She looked at me with this annoyed stare and said, "I'm good." With that comment, she literally walked away from me. *Awkward.*

The conversation ended so quickly, while still standing there processing the strange interaction. It was obvious these people didn't need or even want any help.

Walking out of the front door, I glanced at their business sign to ensure I was at the right place!

Later that evening, after reflecting on a day filled with handwritten invoices, a dirty nursery that smelled like a bar, an old cash register and two meetings I thought to myself. *What did I just get myself into?* In honoring my commitment to Kevin, I typed up some letters for the two businesses to send out to their customers explaining their merger, and then said a prayer for him. It was obvious why Kevin was completely overwhelmed with the entire process. In just the few hours of observation, I was overwhelmed!

A couple of months after the merger was completed, Kevin asked me to stop into the nursery and meet with him, his office manager, and the now previous nursery owners. They had finally gotten moved into the nursery and were beginning operations together after the legal portion was finalized. We had not talked since he asked me to visit both of the businesses, so I wasn't sure how everything had finally come together.

After walking into the nursery to meet with everyone, Kevin led me back to an office area where the group was sitting. This time, the husband of the not-so-friendly lady greeted me, introducing himself as the previous owner of the nursery. We had just sat down when the realization hit me as to why it smelled like a bar in that building. There sat the previous owner with a fresh cigarette lit in an ash tray on his desk. *I am pretty sure that is not legal anymore.*

The tension in the room was immense, but thankfully, my preparation for the meeting paved the way for some constructive conversation. While explaining a marketing plan and ways they could start merging everything for the customers to see, the group began collaborating about how to implement some of the ideas just discussed. By the time the meeting was over, everyone seemed to be a little more relaxed. Despite the meeting ending well, it was still obvious Kevin was in WAY over his head.

A month later, while processing the news of my fourth (and final) pregnancy, Kevin asked for my help in assisting his office manager with some office work, while he went to his mother's funeral in Wisconsin for a few days. We agreed for me to check in with her the following day to see where she could use my assistance.

As promised, the next day I met his office manager at the nursery, and she gave me a rundown of where everything was. With having little knowledge about their operations, it seemed easiest for her to just plug me in where it would benefit her the most. Everything was honestly such a mess.

Literally, with stacks of stuff everywhere, it was easy to feel sorry for her—she seemed completely overwhelmed. Noticing a stack of checks on her desk, I asked her if they were payments to be applied to customer accounts, which she confirmed. She immediately began showing me how to process them in their system, which seemed easy enough.

The reality was that it was a complete struggle to stay focused on that task alone through the piles of paperwork, clipboards, binders, and unopened stacks of mail. In addition, she was running a loud dot-matrix machine that was printing off a stream of carbon-copy invoices. While waiting for her to give me another project, I started looking through their computer program and noticed it had the capability to route and send e-statements.

Over the loud printer, we began discussing the capability of the software system, questioning the ability to send customers e-statements, instead of printing out carbon copy invoices to then get organized by route. She told me that function of the software did not work, which didn't make any sense. *Why would a software offer a capability that didn't work?*

While waiting for her to give me another task, I did a quick search of their program, which appeared that the function could work; it just needed to be set up by an IT professional. After explaining my observation, we agreed for me to have one of my IT friends look into it further. Beginning that process alone could easily save considerable office time, and it was obvious she needed more time to get everything done effectively.

In visiting with her while we worked on a few small projects, she told me about how she was currently splitting her time between helping in the office there, and working in Kevin's wife's shop, where she owned a business as well. In looking at the stacks of clutter, we both agreed that the office needed someone full time to keep up with its demands. She admitted that she would prefer to be in the office full time, but confessed she just went where she was told.

The next morning, I waited nearly 45 minutes for his office manager before realizing she was obviously running late. In thinking about my promise to help in the office, I began going through the stacks of mail and pulling out the checks to post and prepare for her, since she already showed me how to do that. There were stacks of invoices to get filed in the binder, so the rest of my time was spent working on that.

The office cell phone rang at least 30 times in the two hours spent in the office that morning. At one point, I considered answering the phone and taking messages, but knew that would just create more stress by worrying about how to handle the customers properly. With that thought, it seemed like a better option to let the calls go to voicemail. It was difficult leaving there knowing there was so much to get done, yet not a clue of what to do. My promise felt like such a bust, especially since his office manager never showed up that day. *I have totally failed this guy!*

Kevin arrived back from his trip, and after he got settled, we agreed to meet to go over my observation in his office. It was obvious that "business train" would be derailing very quickly if there wasn't a plan put in place soon. In giving him a rundown of my observations, my suggestion to hire his office manager full-time was cut short, as he told me how he just fired her. *Why in the hell would he do that?* There was an enormous rush in my chest as he continued to tell me how he just didn't trust her, and he was following his gut to remove her from the business.

In looking at the obvious mess and disorganization in the office, how could he not see the dysfunction, and just let her go without any plan? There were no words to describe the amount of stress I felt, worrying that this hard-working man was going to have a heart attack if he kept operating with knee-jerk reactions. In discussing the office mess, he said he would have his nephew take it on, since he had good computer skills. Having computer skills was just a small fraction of what that office needed.

Despite his confidence, my chest hurt worrying about the success of his business with so much falling apart. This business was a complete wreck. Remembering how Kevin initially contacted me, needing guidance for marketing, it was obvious this business was nowhere near ready for more customers. The current customers were a complete blessing to that company, let alone adding new ones! *I don't think I have the patience to tackle this amount of disorganization!* By this point, my plate was completely full juggling pregnancy fatigue, my family, and a full-time career. In explaining my limited schedule, he just smiled and insisted it would all work out.

Over the next couple of months, in between my busy work schedule, I stopped in the office to check in with Kevin and his nephew. Since cash flow was essential for business success, preparing the deposits became my top priority. Whenever inquiring about the billing, Kevin usually dismissed it as being under control, though in the back of my mind it seemed questionable.

Nearly each week, Kevin would ask me if my interest of becoming a business partner had changed. The conversation usually ended with me dismissing his offer as a joke and nothing serious. Despite his desperation for help, there was no way he could afford to match my salary at that time.

One thing that was evident early on was that Kevin was a moving target, and very difficult to reach. He was always in production mode, running sunup to sundown. Remembering how he liked to work out at the gym, it seemed easy to set up a time to meet and work out, while we discussed ways to get the office organized and more efficient. During those workouts, he would also utilize the time to educate me about the industry, since there wasn't anyone there to collaborate with to help me fully understand everything.

After a couple of months, I quickly noticed that the number of checks coming in each week was decreasing. When going through customer accounts, there wasn't a lot being billed out, yet the crews were going out in the field doing something almost daily. *How are they logging all the work they do?* At this point, despite my initial thought, it was probably good that the previous owners of the nursery agreed to stay on to help him, as two businesses operating at this capacity would have been financially draining.

In observing all of this, it was easy to feel so bad for Kevin, especially knowing how he was such a hard-working man. This poor man worked so hard to make sure production was done yet failed to recognize the importance of making time to bill out his production. I knew he had no idea that he was basically donating his time to his customers, since they were not getting billed for the services provided.

By that point, I was nearly five months pregnant and struggling to juggle a full-time career and helping Kevin with his two businesses. My mind was in overload trying to focus on so many moving pieces. It reached a point where I couldn't stop thinking about what all needed to be done for the success of the businesses. I started looking at my full-time career, and thinking, maybe it was time to look at other options. With that thought, maybe it was time to take Kevin up on his many offers—and at that point he was begging—for me to help him run the businesses.

In discussions with my husband about the situation, he pointed out my months of involvement of ensuring the success of the merger proved where my heart was, so it just made sense to go full-time. After thinking it over, I called Kevin and shared my interest in his business proposition of joining him to get everything organized and more efficient.

There was no doubt in my mind he just dropped what he was doing…he was at my house within minutes to discuss the idea in detail. He ended up eating dinner with my family that night, and our dinner discussion was all about ideas for the business. Even the kids had ideas about what we should do.

Since the industry was fairly new to me, I made a list of everything that needed to be done right away, in which he would need to assist me. I negotiated a salary, which was ultimately a pay cut for me, but knowing the business would be a success, we could re-negotiate an increase when it was feasible. He even acknowledged he was struggling financially; however, he assured me he would adjust my salary once the company could afford it. As soon as he left, the rest of my evening was devoted to preparing my resignation letter, which I planned to deliver to my boss the very next morning.

That resignation wouldn't be as easy as planned. After hand-delivering my resignation letter to my boss, he begged me to reconsider. From his perspective, it was difficult to understand why I would want to leave my position after answering all of his questions. There weren't any issues with leading my project. There was nothing negative going on with my team. It wasn't about the money. By the end of our hour-long conversation, I somehow agreed to help out until they found my successor, with no idea when that would be.

Leaving that meeting, it was unclear of what I had actually accomplished! I was still working two jobs, except now my new full-time job was a reduction in pay, and without benefits. In addition, I was committing myself to working part-time with my current employer at an hourly rate. In my mind, agreeing to still manage the project, and submit reports might be a good thing in the event there was a need to change directions later if necessary. Despite the change in career status, my excitement was barely contained. Even though it was unclear of what I had just taken on, my gut was telling me it was the right choice.

My first couple of days full time in the office were days that will never be forgotten. Right away, the list of things that needed to be organized and managed grew, starting with billing. My assumptions were spot on about the cash flow issue, as invoices had not been sent to customers in over three months. As a customer, I couldn't even imagine receiving an invoice for a service three months late, nor receiving multiple invoices for reoccurring services. My head hurt thinking about the phone ringing with angry customers.

In addition to the billing issue, Kevin gave me access to the company bank account, so that the past due invoices could get paid. He was still handwriting checks out, which floored me. Thinking of how we could save time by not writing out a ton of checks, I told him we could get all of the vendors set up through the online bill payment, which also allowed us to track the status of payments and annual operating totals.

Once getting logged into the company's bank account, I about fell to the floor at the realization there was less than five thousand dollars in the business checking account. In scrolling through the ridiculous amount of transactions, I was so confused. It looked like someone had literally gone on a shopping spree, as there were so many transactions for retail stores. *Did he give me access to the wrong bank account?*

After my confirmation of the correct bank account, I was still trying to absorb it all. There were more than thirty thousand dollars in invoices, and there wasn't even enough money in the account to cover the small amount of payroll due by the end of the week.

The mowing and spraying crews were in and out of the office that morning grabbing stuff. They looked like they just got out of bed, wearing dirty holey tee shirts and jeans. They were so loud and obnoxious when discussing their wild night running from the police. *Am I hearing this correctly, they were running from the police?*

Just a few days prior, I was wearing a business suit, working with college educated colleagues, who had doctorates and master's degrees, even retired Army colonels and lieutenant colonels. Now, I found myself trying to understand a conversation between two co-workers who had just gotten out of jail, and were educating me on "popping cherries," and "blow-blow systems in their cars" while they shared their jailhouse experiences. To say there was a bit of culture shock was every bit an understatement. I felt like such an idiot. *What were popping cherries and blow-blow systems?*

Later, while trying to understand the checking account chaos, one of the vendors called the office phone—which never stopped ringing, by the way—demanding to collect payment over the phone, or he was ceasing any future purchases. *Holy nightmare!* The next ten minutes were spent explaining the situation of how I was there to get everything organized, all the while re-assuring this vendor that we would get a payment out by the end of that week. I was still unsure what that vendor was for, but his conversation led me to believe it was a vital part of the business. Getting a payment by the end of the week would be a stretch since the checking account was nearly drained.

In between the constant phone ringing, I found the passcode to go through the thirty-something voicemails on the phone. Most people were asking when they would get a bill from us. Halfway through the voicemails, there was a voicemail from Kevin's accountant asking to get copies of specific documents from two years ago, so she could finish the tax preparation for that year. *Two years ago?* Looking at a calendar to confirm what year we were in, maybe she said the wrong year in her message? *The mess just keeps coming at me!*

Opening the file drawers was a mistake. There were literally file folders of unopened mail just stuffed in them. These file folders made any person's junk drawer look like a plate of cookies. Still trying to wrap my mind around everything, I opened all of the mail and started sorting in piles. The scary ones coming from state departments and the Internal Revenue Service were my obvious priority.

While answering the office phone in between finishing up the file drawer clutter, I took a call from Kevin's wife, who was basically accusing me of sleeping with her husband. *Seriously? Am I being punked?* I ended my first week with a ton of tears, convincing myself it might be best to walk away. Better yet, run!

That evening, there were a ton of tears while discussing my crazy week with my husband. My mind was in complete overload, re-capping the week of non-stop phone-ringing, stacks of unopened mail, thirty-some voicemails, drained bank accounts, taxes not being filed, and basically being called an "unmentionable" name. This was all going on while working on a hot summer day in

June, six months pregnant, and in a building that wasn't air-conditioned.

There was a nonstop flood of tears while questioning my career choice. I was completely convinced I had made the biggest mistake of my life. He honestly had more faith in me or was just plain scared of his hormonal pregnant wife, as he said, "If anyone can tackle such dysfunction, it's you." Tackling this mess felt as if I had walked into a hoarder's home and trying to figure out where to begin the clean-up.

Ingredient
Honoring Commitments

AFTER MY HEART FOUND its way back into my chest, it made sense to do what I seem to do well: develop a plan. Since the commitment was made, there was no reason to analyze why the choice to commit was even made. I would rather re-focus my energy and tackle the mess that had been discovered. Obviously, there was a ton of chaos to work through, but it was time to confront the mess and move on. After all, one doesn't purchase a home, then pack up when the roof starts to leak and the basement floods.

My notebook of plans became my life for the next couple of months. My first priority was to get some money flowing back into the business. Next up was combing through every drawer and file in that office, until every piece of paper had been previewed and given some sort of designation. Kevin and I then made a list of all the outstanding invoices along with due dates, so we could figure out which invoices took priority. We implemented a budget and made calls to set up payment plans. There were so many prayers said, each asking for the patience to help me get through the stress.

Kevin agreed to limit all transactions through the business accounts, to strictly necessary business purchases. With that said, it was imperative for him to help me take appropriate steps to follow the plan we agreed to, no matter how much change it required. He clearly acknowledged the prior system wasn't working, so adapting to change was the only way to see success.

Kevin would have four or five new estimates to run each day, which became very time consuming, and half the time he would take a week to get them completed. We came together and figured out a price per square footage. Once I had that, I was able to utilize the internet to figure out a rough estimate of square footage for turf, which then allowed me to complete the estimates. All of that allowed the turnaround time to be almost within 24 hours from the initial request to customer review.

In addition to working crazy hours to get everything organized with the business, cramming before my baby's due date, I was still managing the military historian project that I tried to leave behind when I first agreed to join Kevin. My time was limited to only ten hours per week, devoting the majority of that time to checking in with my team, and getting all weekly reports submitted to my boss.

Nearly three months after starting the new business adventure, while at a weekly maternity appointment, my doctor told me to plan a delivery date to get induced. That date was scheduled just two weeks away, which with everything I had going on, felt like one day away. Scheduling that delivery date meant it was time to call my part-time boss, and officially hand everything off to my successor. Within a couple of days, my final report was submitted, and I turned in my badge and laptop to officially end that chapter of my career.

The last two weeks were spent organizing Kevin's office, scheduling invoices for payment, getting payroll figured out, and coordinating the routes for the guys while I was going to be out of the office. My induction was scheduled on a Monday, so Sunday evening was devoted to getting all of the deposits ready in preparation for my days away from the office. Before leaving that evening, I left instructions for Kevin to not let anyone touch anything until my return!

The following day, my fourth and final baby, Bryce, was born. Bryce didn't realize that day how he would become my new office assistant. Leaving the hospital on Wednesday, my husband drove Bryce and I to the office, where we worked for a couple of hours until the kids arrived home from school.

There were times of regret for not taking a maternity leave to soak up my last baby; however, being able to take him to the office for nearly five months, allowed us to have tons of bonding time. Thankfully, he was born just before the winter season, which afforded me the luxury of soaking up time with him during the business' non-seasonal period.

Being that it was wintertime, Kevin often took Bryce and played with him while I jammed away on everything. Prior to Bryce's arrival, Kevin told me I had to have a girl, as he wasn't good with boys after raising three daughters. He couldn't have been more wrong about that statement— those two are absolutely two peas in a pod! Through the years in the business, Kevin has taught Bryce how to run most of the equipment. Honestly, every six-year-old needs a 53-year-old best friend!

Those first winter months were also used to work with the accountant to get the back taxes figured out. Many tears were shed when the accountant said the business owed over sixty-five thousand dollars, particularly when recalling how much time was just spent in getting all of the outstanding invoices paid. We dove into the next year's list of items needed to process the back taxes, and after a couple of months, another sixty thousand dollars was added to the amount due, now bringing the total to over one hundred and twenty thousand dollars. More tears.

After talking with the accountant, I researched and found a tax attorney to help us get a monumental problem figured out. We worked together to prepare an installment agreement with the IRS so we could remove some of the hefty penalties and interest. Meanwhile, Kevin proceeded to go through a hostile divorce, and was obligated to pay a substantial amount to his ex-wife. Each layer of life in this business called for more planning and organizing, but thankfully it all worked out. We got the IRS paid off within two years, and Kevin reached a final settlement with his ex-wife to remove that weighty monthly burden.

After a full year of getting Kevin's side of the business completely organized and flowing, I hired someone to take it on. My focus then shifted to the nursery and landscape side of the business, in efforts to get it organized. Thankfully, that side of the business was fairly organized; we just needed to update some processes and procedures. We traded in the old cash register for a point of sale system, and we started providing actual invoices to customers instead of a handwritten one.

We implemented an annual fall festival where we had a live band, petting zoo, face-painting, and pumpkin painting. One year, we even had a pie-baking contest. We also featured periodic sales to gain more foot traffic in the nursery. After the first year of getting the nursery in this century, I hired a marketing coordinator to manage all of the website content, Facebook administration, and special events. We were jamming. Our sales were increasing, which meant we were hiring more employees to help.

Nearly three years after we began our business adventure together, Kevin accepted an award from the area chamber of commerce as business of the year. As he received the award, I fought back tears during his acceptance speech, realizing what we had accomplished together through the years. When it's a part of daily routine, one tends to forget the ride along the way.

There were many struggles through those years as we learned to balance out a partnership. We also faced the rumors of us having romantic involvement, which was just annoying in itself. Anyone who was paying attention could see the direction the business was going, and that was our only focus—not a romantic relationship. Thankfully, we were both able to ignore the negative energy, and continue to grow the business into a respectable workplace.

Four years later, we purchased six acres in a neighboring town where we launched a new name and logo to officially bring the two companies together. We accepted the risk, moving nearly eight miles down the road. It proved to be a successful purchase. We currently employ seven full-time salaried positions, and during the season have nearly fifty employees.

When Kevin first purchased the nursery, the combined gross income from the two businesses was around nine-hundred thousand. Six years later, we grossed over two-million and almost all of the company debts are paid, including the land and building. We have an amazing team that is dedicated to continued success.

Nearly a year and half ago, we officially signed papers for equal ownership. Being able to wake up nearly every day excited about going to work is so rewarding. Not only am I grateful for the team we have created, but also truly love every aspect of the business. If someone would have asked me ten years ago if I would ever own a turf management, landscaping and retail nursery, my response would have quickly ended that conversation in laughter.

My drive for this success was the commitment made to a new friend. Often times there have been thoughts about how different things would be if I didn't stop for gas that morning on my way to work. Something led me to make that particular stop that specific morning, which led to my ultimate business success. The amazing outcome is something for which I will always be grateful, as well as gaining a new best friend with whom to partner.

The Recipe

WITH EACH SITUATION IN life, there is an outcome, and that outcome is a reflection of choices. Choices are fueled by many ingredients, such as motivation, determination, ambition, and even commitment. If the outcome isn't what was meant to be achieved, then the processes along the way have to be changed, as well as the attitude towards the desired outcome.

For me, as I have fully disclosed, life brought me many challenges, or bad lemons. Some of the choices I made through situations haven't always made me proud, but I'm grateful for learning I had the power to fix them. At a minimum, my perception towards something could easily be changed, and that was alone was always uplifting.

In 2015, I shared coffee with a social worker in efforts to determine how I could make a difference for foster children, whether it be through volunteer work or some form of mentorship. During that meeting, we discussed the statistics of success for foster kids, which was mind-blowing to me. She shared that less than five percent of foster children cycle out of poverty, drugs, and abuse. *Five percent? How can that be possible?*

After that meeting, that unfortunate statistic was forever stuck in my mind. In just reviewing my own situation, realizing that out of my two sisters and myself, I was the only one to graduate high school and continue on to graduate college. We each had a different path to achieve our personal success. For me, being adopted by a family living in a trailer park, to running a $2.2 million company,

I somehow found the ingredients for a sweet pitcher of lemonade, despite all of the bad lemons given to me.

Thankfully, I figured out early in my years a kind of wisdom that didn't require me to watch and wonder. It doesn't matter why a person has what they have. The important thing to me was what I was going to do to get what I wanted? And if the initial plan didn't work, guess what? There's a "next" plan. It was all in how badly I wanted it.

Although it's easy to forget, I do my best to focus on gains, instead of my losses, which I have learned people often forget. My tire may be flat on my car, but I have a vehicle. There might be a leak in my basement, but I have a place to come home to every day. My kids can be defiant, but I am able to have kids. My family may not be traditional, but I have amazing friendships. My scale might be up ten pounds, but I can change my diet and increase my exercise. My friend might be in a negative funk, but I can choose to lift that friend up, or find another friend.

In the end, the choice is mine, and I can only control MY choices. My choice is to continue to make lemonade with all of the bad lemons.

Acknowledgements

As a child, I knew I aspired to rise above. I didn't really know what that meant at the time, but just knew I had to cycle out of the life that didn't seem to fit me. Some may call it ambition; however, I call it my destiny. The bad lemons I received became a lifeline of sorts. They provided an opportunity for me to defy the odds. Making sweet lemonade from each bad lemon was my way of cycling out of the moments that truly made me feel stuck.

Over time, I realized that I could make a difference, and by sharing my story could encourage others to reevaluate their existence, and not be defined by circumstances often beyond one's control. My story could be like someone else's story that, perhaps, felt trapped by lack of motivation and determination.

I always knew that I wanted to write a book, but I do think I owe much of this inspiration to those who encouraged me to reach out and breathe some positive life. When I first decided to write a book, I thought of how I would put so many thoughts on paper about my personal experiences with "bad lemons." Thank you to those who gave me the confidence to open up and share my personal recipes in dealing with such bad lemons.

A special thanks to my daughter, Grace, for constantly asking me when I was going to make this happen. We were sharing a special day, talking about writing about my personal experiences, when the title blurted out of my mouth. It stuck from then on, and I knew it would continue to inspire me to tell my story.

To my children, Grace, Jack, Luci and Bryce, my reasons for living and finding the right recipes. I obviously never knew what it meant to be a mother, but I knew I wanted to be the mother that I always wanted, yet never had. Life will naturally bring tough days; however, I hope the ingredients will be remembered when life delivers bad lemons. I love you from the deepest part of my heart.

To my grandparents, John and Wilma, for always being my driving force, and constantly encouraging me to be a good person. You both will forever hold a place in my heart.

To my adoptive parents, Cheryl and Floyd, for giving me a home and family when I had neither. And for allowing me the opportunity to share a piece of my life with my sister again. As a mother, I know that decision didn't come easy.

To my biological sisters, wishing you both the happiness we all three deserve. God has watched over us and given us strength to find our desired paths.

To the positive women in my life, who are my sisters from other mothers, Cindy, Mandy, Michele, and Heather. You have listened to my tears and anxieties over the years yet empowered me and gave me strength. I love you all from the bottom of my heart.

About the Author

GIVING UP HAS NEVER been an option for Angie Hundley. She has overcome an array of circumstances and events that would leave many others lost and in despair.

Angie used each negative circumstance in her life to fuel her drive to be more than the low success rates for foster children would allow. In her debut book, *A Recipe for Bad Lemons*, Angie gives a glimpse of what determination and grit can get you. The most remarkable thing about Angie is that she never doubted for a moment that she would create the successful life that she dreamed of—even if that dream looks different than she originally expected.

Angie is a mother of four children and spends her time passing on important lessons to her children. She actively teaches by example. When adversity comes her way, she rolls with the punches and looks for opportunity. Her greatest opportunity thus far presented itself during a fateful meeting with an old friend who later became her business partner of a successful multi-million dollar per year business. When Angie was a little girl in the throes of the foster care system, after being molested by her mother's boyfriend and later abandoned by her mother, she never anticipated just how successful she would become.

The lessons Angie shares are poignant and adoptable. If you have ever thought that you couldn't be more than the adversity you are currently in, then get to know Angie. Connect with her on her website, www.angiehundley.com or on social media. Angie's perseverance and resilience will inspire you and perhaps be just the motivation you need to make your own batch of lemonade!

This hard-working lemonade-maker enjoys working out, baking, and spending time with her kids and friends. In her spare time, she loves travelling to her vacation home to soak up the serenity of the ocean.